FIVE LOAVES,

TWO FISH,

TWELVE

VOLUNTEERS

GROWING A RELATIONAL
FOOD MINISTRY

ELIZABETH MAE MAGILL

UPPER
ROOM BOOKS®
NASHVILLE

To the members of the Worcester Fellowship leadership team.
Thank you for teaching me how to lead.

CONTENTS

Acknowledgments 7

Introduction 9

PART ONE: PEOPLE AND FOOD

Chapter One: Feeding Jesus 21

Chapter Two: Problems with Direct-Service Charity 32

Chapter Three: Listening 43

PART TWO: LET THEM LEAD

Chapter Four: Cultural Conflict 59

Chapter Five: Everyone Can Volunteer 69

Chapter Six: Leadership Teams 88

Chapter Seven: Let Volunteers Lead 98

Chapter Eight: Living with Chaos 107

Chapter Nine: Unexpected Learnings 119

CONTENTS

PART THREE: CREATE CHURCH

Chapter Ten: Interdependence 129

Chapter Eleven: Creating Networks 143

Chapter Twelve: Eating Together Is Church 154

Conclusion: Go Out into the World 165

Churches Mentioned 169

For Further Reading 171

Notes 172

ACKNOWLEDGMENTS

How can I acknowledge all the people who have made my work possible? This only can be the start of that work.

For my writing, I give thanks to Mary Nilson, who suggested that I could learn to make better sentences, and to the Collegeville Institute, who allowed me to work with Mary. Thank you to Russell Dalton and Brite Divinity School for believing I had something to say and for guiding me steadily toward saying it. Thank you to the Louisville Institute Pastoral Study Project Grant, which gave me the funding to extend my research and to sit down and write. Thank you to Charlene Smith, the writing teacher who was willing to say, "This is boring," therefore guaranteeing that readers would get stories instead of theological babbling. Thank you to Beth Storrs, who loved my project and read draft after draft after draft.

For the experiences that led to writing this book, I give thanks to my husband, Ken Porter, who insisted that he always wanted to be married to a doctor—and then to a writer. I thank Mary Jane Eaton and Georgeanne Bennett, who made Worcester Fellowship what it is. Thank you to my parents, Ruth and Charlie Magill, whose "Faith without works is dead" cross-stitch hung in our dining room as I was growing up.

A special thank-you goes to all the volunteers and staff at the food pantries, meal programs, and gardens where I visited. Thank you for sharing your experience and wisdom with me. Your work has lifted me up, given me hope, and reminded me again and again of my faith in the love that God has shared with us.

INTRODUCTION

Alan annoyed me from the first day I met him. He wore oversized shoes, a too-small coat, worn-out jeans, and a severe look on his face. I wore a church dress, a fitted jacket, a smile, and a stole that proclaimed my ecclesiastical authority. He was in his early fifties, just like me. He grew up in an all-white neighborhood like mine, where dads worked nights and moms stayed home with children or worked secretarial jobs. As kids, we both were taught that we could succeed in life. I went to college, earned a bachelor's degree, a master's degree, and later a doctorate. Alan worked retail. When I met him, he didn't have housing or a job. An alcoholic, he lived at the bus station. He had a "don't tell me what to do" attitude. I owned a house in the suburbs, was the part-time pastor of an outdoor church, and didn't want to be told what to do either.

Alan and I met on a Sunday at Worcester Fellowship, an outdoor church in Massachusetts for people who don't have homes or are food insecure, where I ministered to people in the lunch line. Alan waited in the cold with a hundred others for a peanut butter and jelly sandwich and a bag of chips. He showed up sometime after the city built an ice rink on the downtown common. Worcester Fellowship held its lunch and worship time at the corner of the common farthest from the skaters.

Worcester Fellowship's volunteers piled boxes full of sandwiches and garbage bags full of new white socks on the folding table that we used as an altar after distributing lunch. Alan, like most of Worcester Fellowship's members, was considered "very food insecure" by the people who make such delineations, meaning he didn't have regular access to food outside of meal programs like Worcester Fellowship. In addition to being "food secure," I had the power to enforce rules upon the people filing past me to eat.

From his first day at Worcester Fellowship, Alan began pulling me aside to complain about how I handled the lunch line, to point out something missing from his lunch bag, to criticize the upcoming worship service, to tell me with a drunken slur that people were stealing socks. As his pastor, I felt that I needed to respond with a pleasant, conversational tone and a listening ear, but I found myself irritated, and it showed.

WORCESTER FELLOWSHIP

In 2006, years before Alan showed up, my co-pastor, Mary Jane Eaton, and I walked the streets of Worcester, getting to know people hanging out in the parks and on the street corners. Worcester is a working-class city not quite an hour west of Boston, whose population is a majority white, almost a third Hispanic, and about a tenth African American. Worcester also boasts a small but rapidly growing Asian American community. The downtown area is overwhelmed by a small convention center and a large hospital. Small businesses and studio apartments struggle along several blocks of Main Street.

The first meeting at Worcester Common on Easter Sunday 2007 gathered six people for worship and lunch; by the second year, the church was feeding sixty to one hundred adults each week. Worcester Fellowship, which is affiliated with the United Church of Christ (UCC) and Christian Church (Disciples of Christ, or DOC), operates like an indoor church—that is, a church that has a building. It offers Sunday worship and Bible study, midweek programs, prayer teams, a book discussion group, leadership retreats, and a craft circle. Unlike most churches, Worcester Fellowship has no building. Members worship outdoors, and parishioners, visitors, and volunteers eat lunch together every Sunday. Although the church takes a weekly offering, most of the funding comes from other churches, individual donors, and grants.

Worcester Fellowship was five years old when its board sent me to City of God, a conference in Washington, D.C., for members of downtown churches in various cities to come together and wrestle with how to be more involved in the challenges of the cities where they serve. After visiting a variety of outreach ministries in the capital, the workshop leaders asked attendees to reflect on what our home congregations could do to engage more fully with our city. I knew Worcester, and I knew my congregation. But I didn't know the answer. Worcester's primary mission activity was lunch, but I'd never let any members of the congregation help serve the meal. Members of indoor churches in Worcester were recruited to hand out lunch, which the outdoor Worcester Fellowship members ate. The question about outreach led me to an embarrassing realization: I wasn't letting the members of Worcester Fellowship take part in our ministry.

I'd read the liberation theology of Gustavo Gutiérrez and agreed with his argument that people can be trusted to lead the activities they need. I'd studied community organizing and Marshall Ganz's theory that each community has its own story and its own leaders. I'd taught courses on the theology of lay ministry and explored how congregations can do ministry without paid clerical leadership. I dutifully noted that ministers are "the people of the congregation" on the bulletin of indoor churches I pastored. I was part of the Living Stones Partnership in the Episcopal Church, which states that baptism calls everyone to ministry. Even so, I found myself here: a pastor who didn't let her parishioners engage in ministry.

Once home from the conference, I reported my discovery to Mary, and we began to outline a new approach. We created a worship planning meeting to assign the tasks of handing out food and socks, to choose leaders for distributing Communion, to assign scripture passages to readers, and to find leaders for the prayers. We tried to choose about half our volunteers each week from the outdoor congregation and half from the visiting indoor congregation. We selected outdoor volunteers we thought would remain calm and gracious and wouldn't overreact to complaints and had the personal strength to prevent people from taking more than one of each item. We asked indoor volunteers without other responsibilities to stand in the lunch line, select a sandwich, find someone they had not met, and listen to his or her story. Youth visitors were assigned the task of learning our parishioners' names. We wanted everyone to eat together and for all of us to get closer to one another and to God.

The result was chaos.

Outdoor parishioners were confused by our intent and quick to anger if we did not assign them a volunteer slot. Volunteers from indoor churches were afraid to stand in line and wouldn't take a lunch, saying, "It's for *them*." They ended up standing around behind the distribution table talking to one another. One week, two volunteers screamed at each other over who had responsibility for socks and sandwiches—one arguing that the other always got to hand out sandwiches, and it was his turn now; the other accusing him of giving extras to his favorite people. Week after week, people in the lunch line accused the volunteers distributing the sandwiches of stealing. One or two people from indoor churches pulled me and Mary aside to explain that they'd spent hundreds of dollars to provide these meals—didn't we know how much juices boxes cost?—so why weren't they allowed to hand them out?

I was frazzled and defensive when Alan appeared in the lunch line that cold, snowy afternoon.

"You know," he said from the lunch line, "you're doing this all wrong."

Oh really? Do you have a better idea? I wondered angrily but silently. Aloud, I laughed and said, "We sure are! Come to our planning meeting next week and sign up to volunteer."

Alan didn't come to the planning meeting. But he continued to show up at lunch, sometimes a little tipsy, sometimes very drunk, always chatting with those around him. Over time, he shared bits about himself—that he was out of work, that he wasn't willing to sleep at a shelter, and that he knew how to organize things. Alan never admitted to being homeless, but others in the community told me he slept at the bus station. He pulled me aside week after week with his evaluation of Worcester Fellowship's ministry.

"This isn't working," Alan said one day. "People are going to steal all this food."

"It's free," I reminded him. "How can they steal it?"

"People are taking you for a ride," he continued. "They can go to the Salvation Army. They are taking advantage of you."

"Well, we're offering another option. And the Salvation Army is not open for lunch on Sundays."

"But not everyone stays for church," Alan countered.

"You don't come to worship either, Alan. It's not required." After conversations like these, I would move down the serving line to avoid him. I was exasperated with him and mad at myself for being exasperated. I felt I was failing at being pastoral with him. Worcester Fellowship's ministry was to listen to and affirm people wherever they were in their journey. I balked at his critiques and let my annoyance show.

One day, Alan's conversation changed. "I think I get it. You are just handing out sandwiches to be nice. You don't care if people who have enough food take a lunch." He paused. "But you are really disorganized, you know." The next week, he showed up early and supervised unloading the lunches from the church van and then rifled through the bags. It was a bitterly cold day, and his dark blue coat was open. He wore neither gloves nor a hat.

"What are you doing?" I tried to keep my voice from sounding judgmental.

Alan looked me in the eye and replied, "Picking out two of each kind of sandwich to save for after church. You always have people come after church asking for sandwiches."

As much as I didn't want to admit it, Alan was right. Saving some sandwiches was a good idea. The other volunteers made space for his sorting. His friendly chatter made the indoor-church volunteers comfortable. The next week, Alan suggested waiting a little longer before inviting people to get a second sandwich. This ensured that people who were late didn't have to wait behind people who had already eaten. A few weeks later, Alan situated the volunteers handing out socks farther from the sandwich queue, and the line moved better.

Then, Alan put a volunteer at the head of the line to hand out plastic bags for people to collect their food and socks. He missed a few weeks after that, explaining when he returned that he'd had a "bit of a binge." Alan never stopped drinking, but he did start hanging around for worship, always off to the side, never part of the circle. When I invited him to participate, he sometimes said he was Jewish. Once, he told me he wasn't religious while setting up the Communion table. He always reminded me to start the opening prayer, and he brought individuals from the park to me, saying, "She'll pray with you" as he walked away.

Months later when someone asked me after church if any sandwiches were left, I said, "Ask Alan," and then I got it. Alan was in charge of lunch.

Alan was better at managing food distribution than anyone else. Volunteers from the indoor churches got to know him and turned to him for advice about details such as how many tuna, bologna, and peanut butter and jelly sandwiches to make. He dealt with fights between the outdoor volunteers, snuck extra servings into the bags of people who were going home to families, and coordinated with the local shelter to distribute leftovers when we had them. He arranged for one of the other Worcester food ministries to bring donations when we ran out. Alan was the brains behind our lunch program.

In many ways, Alan is the brains behind this book. What I learned from Alan led me to a doctoral program and then a Louisville Institute Pastoral Study Project Grant. I visited churches throughout the United States where the people who come for groceries or meals volunteer in the ministry. People like Alan—food insecure, alcoholics or addicts, struggling with mental health challenges—have the skills we need for our food ministries. People with felony records, those unable to look others in the eye, people unreliable with their time all have something to contribute. Opening myself to recognize Alan's organizational skills led me to understanding that church-based food ministries improve when we engage the people we serve with questions about their strengths and gifts and then listen to their answers. Inviting people to help makes our programs better.

UNDERSTANDING THE TERMS IN THIS BOOK

People are hungry. Food insecurity in the United States has held steady since 1995 at 10 to 12 percent of the population[1] or 15 million households in 2017.[2] Meals programs first became a significant part of our culture in the United States with Depression-era soup kitchens. In the late sixties, food banks began collecting food from businesses, individuals, and the United States Department of Agriculture and purchasing food in bulk to distribute to food pantries (programs that give uncooked food to qualifying individuals) and meal programs (programs that cook and serve food).

The history of food programs is one of compassion but not necessarily thoughtfulness as to the best way to help the food insecure. Charity—from Latin *caritas,* or care—was once about loving our neighbor but today is understood as giving our money or resources to others. The Hebrew word for *charity—tzedakah*—connotes righteousness and justice along with

15

distributing the community's resources equitably.[3] The goal of charity is to improve the circumstances of those who lack adequate material resources. Unfortunately, while meeting people's immediate needs, traditional food pantries and meal programs can perpetuate the systems that cause poverty, support stereotypes, and hide the systemic causes of poverty.

To have a conversation about food programs and what they do well and what they can be doing better, we need a common language. I use *people-first* language, naming the humanity of people before an attribute that may describe them. For example, I avoid the word *homeless*; instead I write *people without housing*. People who come to pantries or meals are *people without adequate access to food*. Though this language quickly can become cumbersome in a book about serving people who do not have enough food, I want to be intentional in avoiding the implication that people *are* their circumstance.

SPED

The United States Department of Agriculture (USDA) uses the term *food security* to describe having enough food to be healthy and active. While government subsidies such as the USDA Supplemental Nutrition Assistance Program (SNAP) reduce food insecurity, they do not eliminate it. *Direct-service charities* fill the gap with grocery cards, food pantries, and meals. This book is about church-based food pantries and meal programs. Sixty-two percent of the more than 58,000 pantries and meals in the United States are faith-based.[4]

Although faith-based, most pantries and meals are *transactional*. We can improve them by creating ways for them to become *relational*. Transactional ministry involves an exchange: People with little money are pressured to "earn" access to direct service from church volunteers through correct (generally submissive) behavior and a good story as to how they got into their situation. Relational ministry gets beyond the "good story" to find the real story about what is happening in people's lives and in their faith. It aims to build relationships. Those relationships create *church*. I use the word *church* to mean the not quite explainable experience of local community members as they follow Jesus together rather than a building, a set of beliefs, or an institution.

Shared ministry is the term I use when people who are food insecure and people who are food secure share all aspects of ministry. People who want to donate food or money join in the eating, and people who need additional food resources are encouraged to be volunteers in the program. Shared ministry could include planning, carrying out, and evaluating a church-based food ministry, or it might be sharing tasks such as setting up, serving, and cleaning. Regardless of the work, shared ministry requires volunteers to get to know one another.

I visited church-based food pantries and meals programs that are doing shared ministry based in congregations of thirty to three-hundred members. They are located in Philadelphia and Reading, Pennsylvania; Asheville, North Carolina; Brighton and Boston, Massachusetts; and Pomona, California, and include United Methodist, Episcopal, Evangelical Lutheran, United Church of Christ, and Disciples of Christ denominations. On pages 169–170, I've included a list of the churches, their meal programs and pantries, and the people I met at each location. I imagined shared ministry would create deep and meaningful relationships between people of different classes and races. I imagined shared ministry could fix racism and classism, separation and isolation in our communities. What I found was both less than that and much more.

The stories of the volunteers and church leaders in these ministries provide the guidance we need in order change how we provide food ministry. Part one of this book explores how to hear the voices of people we are serving, part two examines how to make room for the leaders all around us, and part three shows how shared ministry can create a new way to be the church.

DISCUSSION QUESTIONS

1. What do you think of Alan? When in your ministry have you met someone like him?

2. What food security issues are present in the neighborhood your church serves? What programs are already in place?

3. What experience do you have serving at a food pantry or meal program? What was rewarding? What was frustrating?

PART ONE

PEOPLE AND FOOD

ONE

FEEDING JESUS

The title of this book comes from the story of the feeding of the multitudes in John's Gospel. Versions of this story appear six times in the four Gospels: Matthew 14:13-21; Matthew 15:32-39; Mark 6:30-44; Mark 8:1-9; Luke 9:10-17; and John 6:1-13. Each story starts with a large and hungry crowd of four or five thousand and a shortage of food when mealtime comes around. Sometimes the disciples argue about the cost of the bread or the difficulty of getting bread. Clearly, they feel overwhelmed by the task of feeding so many people. Then, somehow five or seven loaves of bread are available, plus some fish. Jesus takes, blesses, breaks, and offers a small amount of bread for the multitudes to share. The miracle is that everyone eats their fill with seven or twelve baskets of food left over.

Two streams of interpretation of these texts exist, the most common being that Jesus' blessing multiplies the bread, reminding us of the manna/bread that God provided for the escaping Israelites in the Exodus story. The second is that this is a miracle of sharing—all those present, seeing Jesus bless the insufficient resources, are moved to take out what they are carrying and share it with those sitting nearby. Regardless of interpretation, Christians everywhere use this story whenever there seems to be not enough, but in the end, there is plenty. There is excess, kingdom-of-God-style excess.

We often miss the role of the people who are hungry and the fact that Jesus does not feed them by himself. There are at least twelve volunteers in the disciples and possibly others from the crowd. I presume the disciples didn't travel with bread baskets for the leftovers, so some people must have offered theirs. In John's Gospel, a boy provides the necessary food to start the meal:

> Jesus went to the other side of the Sea of Galilee, also called the Sea of Tiberias. A large crowd kept following him, because they saw the signs that he was doing for the sick. Jesus went up the mountain and sat down there with his disciples. Now the Passover, the festival of the Jews, was near. When he looked up and saw a large crowd coming toward him, Jesus said to Philip, "Where are we to buy bread for these people to eat?" He said this to test him, for he himself knew what he was going to do. Philip answered him, "Six months' wages [200 denarii] would not buy enough bread for each of them to get a little." One of his disciples, Andrew, Simon Peter's brother, said to him, "There is a boy here who has five barley loaves and two fish. But what are they among so many people?" Jesus said, "Make the people sit down." Now there was a great deal of grass in the place; so they sat down, about five thousand in all. Then Jesus took the loaves, and when he had given thanks, he distributed them to those who were seated; so also the fish, as much as they wanted. When they were satisfied, he told his disciples, "Gather up the fragments left over, so that nothing may be lost." So they gathered them up, and from the fragments of the five barley loaves, left by those who had eaten, they filled twelve baskets. (6:1-13)

I like that the boy doesn't understand that his offering is too little for such a big crowd. The disciples are more realistic, saying something akin to, "How could we ever feed this many people" while the youngster's idealism says, "Do you want the little that I have?" Five loaves are a lot to be carrying around, but maybe the boy has a big family to feed. Or maybe he gathered the food from several families sitting nearby. For some reason, he chooses to give away the food he has. I'm afraid I'm more like the disciples, worried that there are too many hungry people in the world, worried that the enormity of the problem of food insecurity is insurmountable, which leads me to hang on to what little I have. I want to learn to be like the boy who says, "I'll share what I have" even though it is not enough.

I love that the people who feed the crowd—the boy, the disciples, even Jesus—are not food-secure people with excess to give away. The disciples and Jesus are food insecure; they have given up their work to become itinerant preachers who are dependent upon the generosity of others. The crowd is probably mostly day laborers who gave up the chance to earn enough to eat that day. If wealthier people are present, they would have carried at most one day's supply of food with them.

Because of the boy's generosity and Jesus' miracle, there is plenty of food. But the food could not have been distributed without volunteers. In some versions of this story, the crowd is organized into groups of fifty or hundreds of people. The disciples, the boy, and other leaders among the people all choose to help with the food distribution. There is need, yes, but mostly there is a little food and a lot of volunteers. The result is not only that everyone eats their fill but also that there are twelve baskets left over. Not enough becomes a surplus. Five loaves, two fish, and twelve volunteers, blessed by Jesus and his compassion for the people, leads to more than enough food for everyone.

THE JUDGMENT OF THE NATIONS

The most common scripture passage quoted by meal programs and food pantries is the story called the "sheep and the goats" or the "judgment of the nations" found in Matthew 25:31-46:

> "When the Son of Man comes in his glory, and all the angels with him, then he will sit on the throne of his glory. All the nations will be gathered before him, and he will separate people one from another as a shepherd separates the sheep from the goats, and he will put the sheep at his right hand and the goats at the left. Then the king will say to those at his right hand, 'Come, you that are blessed by my Father, inherit the kingdom prepared for you from the foundation of the world; for I was hungry and you gave me food, I was thirsty and you gave me something to drink, I was a stranger and you welcomed me, I was naked and you gave me clothing, I was sick and you took care of me, I was in prison and you visited me.' Then the righteous will answer him, 'Lord, when was it that we saw you hungry and gave you food, or thirsty and gave you something to drink? And when was it that we saw you a stranger and welcomed you, or naked and gave you clothing? And when was it that we saw you sick or in prison and visited you?' And the king will answer them, 'Truly I tell you, just as you did it to one of the least of these who are members of my family, you did it to me.' Then he will say to those at his left hand, 'You that are accursed, depart from me into the eternal fire prepared for the devil and his angels; for I was hungry and you gave me no food, I was thirsty and you gave me nothing to drink, I was a stranger and you did not welcome me, naked and you did not give me clothing, sick and in prison and you did not visit me.' Then they also will answer, 'Lord, when was it that we saw you hungry or thirsty or a stranger or naked or sick

24

or in prison, and did not take care of you?' Then he will answer them, 'Truly I tell you, just as you did not do it to one of the least of these, you did not do it to me.' And these will go away into eternal punishment, but the righteous into eternal life."

This passage leaves me with three questions: (1) who are the "least of these," (2) what does the king mean by "you did it to me" in verse 40, and (3) who is included in "all the nations" that are judged in verse 32?

WHO ARE THE LEAST OF THESE?

In verse 40, the king/judge/Jesus says, "Truly I tell you, just as you did it to one of the least of these who are members of my family, you did it to me." The Greek word for *brothers* is interpreted as "members of my family" because in the first century Christians (both men and women) were thought to be part of a brotherhood. Based on verse 40, the "sheep" took care of Christians in need, making "the least of these" fellow Christians. But in verse 45 "family" is dropped: "Truly I tell you, just as you did not do it to one of the least of these, you did not do it to me." When the New Testament does *not* use family language, the writer is referring to *all* people, not just followers of Jesus.

So which is it? Scholars agree that the point of the text is the importance of helping those who are hungry, thirsty, a stranger, naked, sick, or in prison. Scholars came to this conclusion because both the sheep and the goats are surprised by the results of the judgment. In verse 37, the righteous/sheep say, "Lord, when was it that we saw you . . . ," and the condemned/goats say the same in verse 44. The presumption is that individuals would know if they have gone out of their way to serve the small Christian community. They didn't know, so the "least of these" is all people, regardless of their faith, who need food, drink, clothing, welcome, comfort/healing, and visits in prison.

YOU DID IT TO ME

Next, let's discuss the meaning of the king's words in verse 40: "You did it to me." What does it mean to give food, drink, and clothing *to* Jesus? In the fourth century, John Chrysostom wrote many sermons on Christians' responsibility to care for people who are poor. He believed that interacting with beggars and people who are destitute is a way of engaging with Jesus.[1] Once we presume that Jesus is *in* people who are poor, we see that the poor, like Jesus, have something to offer those of us with material resources. When we find ourselves serving food—a plate of lasagna or a bag of groceries—we can challenge ourselves to imagine that the person before us is Jesus. And if we are serving Jesus, surely we will want to sit down and hear his story.

To be with Jesus is to be with people who are poor; to know Jesus is to know people who are poor. If our reason for serving is to care for the "least of these," then we are called to recognize Jesus in those we serve and to spend the time to build a relationship with them. Jesus is present among people who lack food, drink, and clothing and those who are strangers, sick, and imprisoned. Whenever I find myself thinking that I am an expert on poverty or that people who are poor need my knowledge, I remember that Jesus has more wisdom than I do. Imagine how our relationships with people who are food insecure would change if we assumed they have skills, knowledge, and a particular approach to the world. We must remind ourselves that Jesus is in every person we serve.

ALL THE NATIONS

The story of the sheep and the goats begins with "all the nations" (v. 32) gathered for judgment. In the Bible, "all the nations" is used most often to mean everyone except "us"—that is, everyone except believers. However, scholars have noticed that in this story Jesus is speaking privately to the disciples—not to a crowd—so they must be included in this judgment as well.

Matthew's Gospel was written for a particular congregation of Jesus-following Jewish people and contains the word *church* periodically. Scholars understand this Gospel to be both the story of Jesus' life and instruction for the congregation. Thus, instruction for "the disciples" is also instruction for us as disciples—or Jesus followers. Jesus is speaking to Christians about our judgment and also to all of those who are not with us, "the nations." The judgment is based only on whether the judged gave food to the hungry, drink to the thirsty, clothing to the naked, welcome to the stranger, care to the sick, or visits to the imprisoned. Those who meet the needs of "the least of these" are sheep and blessed with eternal life; those who don't are goats and sent to eternal punishment.

How do the materially poor—"the least of these"—fit into this story? Are they only in the story as a prop, waiting to be served? Does the story intend to communicate that only people who have excess are judged? Are "the least of these" sheep, goats, or something else? One possible reading of this text is that people in need will not face judgment at all; "all the nations" then means those with an excess of material resources, time, and energy. In that interpretation, the people who need material resources, healing, and release from prison serve only as a test for people with enough. Reading the text in this way declares that people with few material resources are fundamentally different from people with plenty. Reading this text as if people living in poverty are not among "the nations" supports the idea that they are less important than those of us with access to material resources. Instead, reading with an eye toward justice requires "all the nations" to include people who also are identified as "the least of these." People with material poverty will be judged based on whether they have helped the hungry, thirsty, the naked, the stranger, and the imprisoned. Jesus calls us all to share with our neighbors.

In my experience people who have no homes and people who are food insecure do not read themselves as missing from this story. Instead, they see the importance of providing help for others in need. People who do not have enough for themselves read this text and want to find ways to meet the needs of others. People in material poverty feel the call to serve food and drink in the same way that people with enough material resources do. Though we recognize the sheep as people who give rather than receive, people who have very little are giving for different reasons than those with much. Persons who are poor are not giving out of excess or as a way to simplify their lives. They want to serve others. Those who are Christian see a simple command from Jesus: Jesus is in those in need, and he asks us to aid other people in need.

Notice also that Jesus' mandate is to care for others without imposing any tests as to whether the help is causing dependence, whether the need is short- or long-term, or even whether the giver feels self-righteous for giving. Judgment only depends on whether a person has provided food, drink, and clothing; welcomed a stranger; cared for a sick person; or visited someone in prison. All people—all the nations, people with and without faith in Jesus, people with and without material resources— need the opportunity to serve others. Food ministries can offer a place for everyone to feed those who are hungry and a chance to serve Jesus.

DID JESUS FEED PEOPLE?

When I began working with Worcester Fellowship, I assumed that to feed other people is to act like Jesus. Christians follow Jesus, and we follow by imitating him. Jesus fed people; we feed people. Serving people who are hungry made me think of Jesus at the head of the table, handing out food. But this is the opposite of Matthew 25 where Jesus says he was *served by* the people being judged. Jesus is the eater, not the server. In the article

"The Hungry Jesus," Andrew McGowan argues that Jesus is more often the guest than the host at the meals described in the Bible:

> Jesus was most clearly someone willing to eat with diverse company, less an inclusive host than an undiscriminating guest. Jesus appears as host only in quite different and more historically contentious material, relative to that where he is depicted as keeping bad company or being a wine-bibber. The "guest" traditions about him are generally defensible; the "host" traditions tend to be more influenced by later reflection than material that scholars in general would actually attribute to the historical Jesus.[2]

As the guest rather than the server, Jesus allows a diverse and less than respectable group of people to serve him. He eats with others more than he serves others. As an itinerant preacher, Jesus engages in the social customs of the communities he visits. He arrives in each location without food, and his hunger opens him to the possibility of sharing a meal with whomever he meets. Because Jesus is often hungry while engaged in ministry, he easily identifies with the people who are hungry in Matthew 25. Thus, we imitate Jesus by eating with people rather than by serving others. But someone still has to serve, right? My solution to this is that we all eat, and we all serve, thereby creating reciprocity in our relationships. Reciprocity requires balance: When someone cares for people in need, people in need care for them.

I've seen this type of reciprocity play out in several different ways. At Worcester Fellowship, I check up on people, and they check up on me. While sitting together at lunch, people asked how I was doing after a car accident or how someone in my family was recovering from an illness. In caring for Jesus in the poor, Jesus in the poor cares for the giver. In the Gospels, Jesus provides healing and teaching for the communities that welcome him with housing and food. Today, Jesus in the poor offers us welcome, conversation, and community. Further, in the effort to look for Jesus in the poor and to let the poor/Jesus care for them, people with material resources begin to recognize the richness of people who need resources. Jesus in the poor opens people's eyes to perceive the world as it is.

Stereotyping makes the work of seeing Jesus in those with few material resources more difficult—even for Christians. I certainly feel uncomfortable imagining Jesus in the violent alcoholic, the prostitute, the person with delusions, the sex offender, or the murderer. It is more comfortable to think of these people as other, as not-like-me, certainly as not-like-Jesus. One practice that helped me to see Jesus in others was to engage in Bible study with the people who came to eat at Worcester Fellowship. Reading the Bible with sex offenders, felons, addicts, and people struggling with mental illness broke down the barrier that I placed between us. I heard their stories of brokenness, and they heard mine. Reading the Bible with people who have few material resources provides a new way to see Jesus in "the least of these."[3]

Ministries that make space to eat and volunteer with people who need material resources make it possible to see Jesus in people in need. Once I recognize Jesus in the person before me, I find myself better equipped to listen to and appreciate his or her story. I trust that Jesus has much to teach me through other people. When I imagine Jesus within a person who is food insecure or who has limited material resources, I see him or her as an equal participant in ministry. And I know that Jesus' presence in others can only improve whatever ministry I am serving. Eating and serving together builds the reciprocity that Jesus modeled. Shared ministry is about welcoming Jesus into ministry with us through the gifts, talents, and offerings of others.

DISCUSSION QUESTIONS

1. What stands out for you in the stories of feeding the multitudes? What lessons can these stories teach you?

2. What is significant about the story of the sheep and the goats? What lessons can this story teach you?

3. How does imagining yourself feeding Jesus as opposed to being Jesus change your perception of food ministries?

TWO

PROBLEMS WITH DIRECT-SERVICE CHARITY

People need food, and we are called by Jesus to provide it to those in need. So what's the problem? Why are so many people food insecure? We know hunger in the United States is caused by poverty, and poverty is a systemic issue caused by job shortages, low wages, the effects of racism and sexism, and insufficient support for people with physical and mental health issues. There is not a shortage of food in the United States but rather a shortage of sharing what we have. Almost all food programs doing the work of sharing food do so using a direct-service approach—meaning people with enough material resources give food or serve meals to people who do not have enough. There are some efforts within direct-service charities to address the systemic causes of food insecurity, but they are rare. Additionally, research tells us that direct-service charities can be harmful to the people they serve. Though my intention is not to place blame or to criticize the work of food ministries, I believe that looking at the potential for causing harm with direct-service charity allows us to improve our strategies.

Direct-service ministries are, by their very nature, inter-personal strategies for dealing with systemic problems. Direct service looks at each individual and meets his or her individual need rather than looking at the system and changing the system that caused the need. Providing food not only does not address the causes of food insecurity but also hides those causes. More-over, offering individuals direct-service charity perpetuates the stereotype that individuals need to be fixed. At the same time, direct-service food ministries may imply that people who volunteer are somehow the model of how to be food secure.

The fact that direct-service charity does not reduce poverty is not a new idea.[1] Although pantries and meals may intend to be short-term solutions to food insecurity, almost two-thirds of households use the programs as ongoing sources of food.[2] With an average household income of $9,900 to $10,800 per year,[3] persons who receive a meal a week or a bag of groceries a month from these ministries are still living in poverty. Food is a stop-gap fix for a long-term, systemic problem, and it is important for churches and church members to take on those systemic issues in order to create any lasting change.

In *Practical Justice: Living Off-Center in a Self-Centered World*, Kevin Blue suggests that there are many different reasons for food insecurity. Using the "teach a person to fish" story, he notes that there are people to whom we need to give a fish, people we need to teach to fish, and systemic challenges to fishing—such as expensive fishing poles and polluted lakes—that no individual can overcome alone. Blue's list of the systemic causes of poverty is extensive: shortages of subsidized housing, the difference in the quality of education in poorer neighborhoods (influenced by the decreased property values and thus lower property taxes), the history of bank and real estate agents engaging in redlining (marking off areas where people of color were allowed to buy homes), the difference in car insurance rates in neighborhoods with minorities, the way the justice system privileges wealth and whiteness, the exploitation of poorer communities with dumps and waste disposal sites, the cost of housing, food, and health care compared to the minimum wage.[4] The people engaged in Worcester Fellowship included persons with disabilities, a small number of persons struggling with addictions, persons with health problems, and persons with part-time minimum-wage jobs. When we provide a fish to people who are overwhelmed by the systemic causes of poverty, we help them for a day but potentially mask or ignore the systemic problems.

DIRECT SERVICE TREATS SOME AS "LESS THAN" OTHERS

Anyone who has gotten to know someone at a meal program or pantry has figured out that people are people: People without access to material resources aren't that different from those of us who have plenty. Yet even when I was spending a lot of time with individuals who were food insecure, I found myself unconsciously buying into the stereotypes about people living in poverty. For example, I was surprised by how many people who need food are white. Only 26 percent of the people who experience food insecurity are African American; 43 percent are white.[5] Other stereotypes include believing that persons living in poverty must be lazy, irresponsible, or unwilling to work.

In *Disrupting Homelessness: Alternative Christian Approaches,* Laura Stivers studies programs working with people who are homeless. She found that volunteers often assumed that the individuals they served needed to be fixed or cleaned up, that they needed a better spirituality, that they were unreliable or incompetent, or that they needed to be taught to work or to follow rules.[6] Those who didn't have homes felt their economic situation and the shortage of affordable housing were the primary causes of their situation.[7] These assumptions then led to the conclusion that providing food or housing gives individuals a crutch when they need a push. Assumptions about food insecurity are similar to those about homelessness. I've often heard said that people who are food insecure "need a hand up, not a handout." The implication is that handouts perpetuate laziness. I've met people who are food insecure who say they want a "hand up" as a way to explain they don't *want* to be going to a food ministry for food.

I never succumbed to believing the laziness stereotype, but I did find myself wondering if people didn't have enough food because of their mental illnesses and addictions. I started to equate significant challenges with mental health, addictions, disabilities, and histories of trauma with food insecurity. Yet many people who have mental illness, addictions, and trauma are not food insecure. My own family includes people with these life challenges, but none of them is food insecure or homeless. While mental illness, addiction, and trauma can lead to reduced financial stability, that isn't always the case. Once I realized this, I started noticing how many of my middle-class friends have addictions and mental illness. I only know of the trauma in the lives of my closest friends, but even that does not lead directly to food insecurity.

My friends and neighbors who live close to the poverty line know how to cook and budget. They don't lack the skills or know-how. What do they lack is a livable wage, access to adequate transportation, and affordable health care. Instead of full-time jobs with benefits, many of them work irregular part-time jobs. Paying for housing takes up a huge percentage of their income, and when emergency expenses arise their food budget suffers. The difference between food secure people with addictions and food insecure people with addictions is *money*. When we say we shouldn't give a person a fish but teach him or her to fish, we presume that the person doesn't already know how to fish. When we try to "fix" or transform the persons who come to our food ministries, we presume that they are damaged and need to be fixed. Yet it's not the damage but the poverty that causes food insecurity. The systems that cause poverty are what need fixing—not the people. When we only focus on transforming a deviant individual, there is a danger of converting more compassionate stereotypes of people in poverty into unfair judgments. We assume that people who are food insecure have nothing to offer those of us who have enough. Even after I understood this concept, I was slow to recognize how Alan knew more about setting up a food line than I did.

Another common judgment of people who eat at meals programs is the test of how "deserving" they are of the help we offer. While people's definitions of who is deserving vary, most believe that children or senior citizens—or perhaps people who have disabilities or mental illness—are the most deserving. Generally, we don't view men of working age as being deserving, especially those who *seem* as if they should be able to work. Even if this is the case, most people who are food insecure *do* have paid work—paid work that is insufficient to lift them out of poverty.

Additionally, as a volunteer at food ministries, my gut reaction is to want to help the people who are grateful, helpful, and good at following the rules. When people are belligerent, demanding, or prone to start fights during a meal, I find it harder to see why I should help them. I don't mean to do it, but my instincts tell me to help those who defer to my authority more than those who ignore rules or protest the ministry's policies—especially if I was one of the persons who created the policies in the first place. I want to believe the rules I set are fair.

Ultimately, direct-service ministries can be problematic because they encourage us to decide who is worthy or unworthy, they classify people as damaged, and they blame people for causing their own dilemmas. The challenge is to change the way we provide direct-service charity so that we don't perpetuate these stereotypes and instead refute them when we notice them in ourselves or in others.

DIRECT SERVICE TREATS SOME AS "MORE THAN" OTHERS

The less recognized stereotype perpetuated by direct-service ministry is the idea that the people who run the ministry—usually volunteers—are "more than" those who eat. Those of us who are food secure might begin to believe that we are more capable at managing food, more adept at navigating life's decisions, or more reliable than those who come to eat. Direct-service charity provides the givers with power and control over other people's meals, and, somewhat understandably, this makes some feel as though they should have power and control over others' lives as well. Some may start believing that they are doing more of what God calls them to do than those who come to eat or pick up food. We have seen a problem and helped to "fix" it, and that can't help but give us satisfaction with ourselves.

Volunteers also have power over the rules and regulations of a particular food ministry, and a desire for order and wanting to be "fair" with what we are giving away may lead us to want to exert power over those people coming into our space. How else will they know the rules? In many programs, breaking the rules of a food pantry means not eating or receiving food for weeks at a time. But whether we have generous policies or strict ones, the power dynamic is clear: People with access to food make the rules, and people with limited access follow the rules. At the same time, the standards we set tend to match the socioeconomic culture in which we find ourselves. We make rules that make sense and seem straightforward to follow for people who are like us. Then when someone fails to follow the rules, it seems to point to a weakness on their part. The rule-makers appear good at order and discipline, and the rule-breakers look like failures. It is only a small step to equate the ability to follow the rules with food security.

As a volunteer, if we take the time to hear people's stories, we may find ourselves wondering why they made particular choices in their lives. We imagine that if the people who need food were just a little bit more like us—a little more willing to follow our rules and guidelines, a little more adherent to our set of values—then they would have adequate material resources in the same way we do. I remember helping a couple move into a new apartment and being horrified to hear how they handled their budget. Essentially, her disability check went to rent; his part-time job paid for utilities, then food, then any other expenses. If he worked fewer hours one month and had a smaller paycheck, they ate more often at the local meal programs. If they had a medical disaster or other need, they reached out to family and local churches for help. At first, I thought they should have a budget like I do and set aside money for unanticipated expenses. After a few years, I realized that they followed their "insufficient" budget better than I have ever followed mine. I had fallen into the trap of believing my wealth was a function of my "better" systems for tracking money.

Direct-service ministry also may imply that those of us with excess food are better than people who are food insecure. This belief begins with good intent: Having extra material resources means a person should give from his or her excess to people who need material resources. The idea seems obvious until we break it down. For example, let's consider clothing giveaways. When we find ourselves with excess clothing, our first thought is *How can I get rid of it?* But is our goal really to clothe others, or is it to clear out our overfilled closets? Food is a different issue. Even food-secure people rarely find themselves wanting to get rid of food items because they are taking up space that could be used for something else. But for those of us who do have more food than is necessary for survival, we want to ease the feeling of guilt caused by that excess. We may want to give the food away, but our main question is who we should give it to. When we separate the two facts—(1) we have too much food and (2) we want to give the food away—we see that excess is the problem and that we are looking for people in need to solve our problem rather than seeing someone else's need and asking how we can help.

The idea that we have material resources to offer others validates our accumulation of those resources. Our materialism begins to look like a virtue instead of the problem that it is. It causes us to focus on our apparent goodness in wanting to give rather than on how unhealthy it is to have acquired excess in the first place. Almost by accident, we see ourselves as more worthy when we give than when we receive. As discussed in chapter one, giving things away seems equivalent to acting like Jesus. Yet in the feeding of the multitudes and in the story of the sheep and the goats, Jesus is not giving away excess. Jesus says that he is in the receivers, not the givers.

While each of us individually may or may not feel "more than" because of our ability to give, giving without receiving creates a power inequity. The givers, as a group, can develop a "god complex."[8] This is the idea that, like God, we have a special ability or special resources that give us the ability to help others. The god complex is a type of dysfunction—we know that it is not okay to see ourselves as more god-like than others—yet we still find ourselves stuck in this way of thinking. A god complex may tell us that our work at a food pantry or meal program proves our worthiness, or it can express itself as pressure to save others or in thinking that saving someone relies solely on us. Some people describe feeling anxious that they are not doing enough to end food insecurity. Certainly, we as a nation should do more, but each of us as individuals is called to work with God, not to be gods. It is the god complex that allows us to stop trusting God and start believing that only we can fill whatever gap we see in the resources of the people we meet. Like poverty, the god complex is a systemic problem that develops from recognizing the economic disadvantages faced by some and feeling the discomfort that arises from the political and religious power that comes with access to resources.

ISOLATION, FEAR, AND OPPRESSION

For the most part we don't like the feeling of superiority that comes with a god complex, and that sense of discomfort makes us avoid situations where we feel it. We end up disconnecting from people rather than working together to dismantle the systems separating us. This results in isolation. Direct-service ministry keeps us separate. In turn, this separation allows fear to fester—the "haves" fearing the "have-nots"—and this fear perpetuates oppression. The segregation of our nation and our church, by race and class, creates a perpetual cycle fed by our fear. Most of us don't know many people who are a different race or class than we are. At most food ministries, the people serving do not live near the people who are eating, which reduces our opportunities to get to know one another as neighbors. The Gospel command to love our neighbors becomes an abstract idea rather than a specific one. As long as we are isolated from one another, we don't understand the lives of those of a different race or class. As long as we don't know our neighbors, our fear keeps us isolated.

While an individual can choose to face his or her fears and break the cycle of isolation, fear, and oppression by seeking out people who are different, oppression is systemic, meaning an individual can resist it but cannot end it alone. Oppression can be based on race, gender, disability, immigration status, education, and more, and all of these parts of a person's identity can contribute to poverty. Classism is oppression based on wealth or income, and it separates people who are food secure from those who are food insecure. Learning to see classism helps us resist it. Seeing classism includes recognizing our role in creating a society where poverty exists. It includes understanding that persons who are poor cannot simply become more like those who are wealthy in order to overcome the systems working against them.

We see classism at work when we assume that people in poverty should assimilate to the culture of people who have enough. A direct-service charity that fails to acknowledge and affirm the differences language and cultural values make on people's lives needs to reevaluate its outreach. As food ministry leaders and volunteers, our challenge is to accept people as they are now, with all the quirks, idiosyncrasies, coping mechanisms, and unusual behaviors they have learned on life's journey and with all the culture and heritage they claim for themselves. It is not helpful to require people to develop a new culture to receive assistance.

One reaction to the systemic nature of poverty is to suggest churches should not engage in direct-service ministry at all. I often hear people saying that churches or faith communities should move away from offering charity and move toward creating justice—that is, toward changing the systems that cause poverty. While I hope churches are engaging in systems change, I contend that ending direct-service food ministry is not a Christian response. While there are serious problems with direct-service charities, hungry people cannot wait until the systems have improved to eat. They need to eat every day, and as Christians we are called to provide that food. Until systems are improved, we are called to provide food for those who are hungry.

Churches should engage in food ministry, providing food in ways that acknowledge the systemic nature of poverty; treating food-insecure individuals as people who have gifts, strengths, and dreams; and recognizing food-secure and food-insecure people as equally loved and in possession of God-given gifts. The primary strength churches bring to food ministry is not their excess of food resources but the excess of Jesus's love, care, and grace and our ability as church members to recognize that all of us need that love, care, and grace regardless of how much food we have. Shared ministry is ministry where everyone can volunteer. Creating shared ministry starts with asking the question "What can we do to serve others?" and trying to answer that question together.

DISCUSSION QUESTIONS

1. What stereotypes have you heard about people who are food insecure? What stereotypes have you heard about people who are food secure?

2. What systemic issues cause poverty in your community?

3. When have you seen yourself or your faith community helping others out of a god complex rather than from a place of equality?

THREE

LISTENING

Volunteers enter from the side entrance of St. James Church, which opens to a shadowy landing with a narrow and decrepit single bathroom to the left, the office door to the right, and stairs lit by a single dull bulb directly ahead. At the top of the stairs, a large, well-lit social hall bustles with activity. Meals take place in this room almost every day. It is worn but welcoming. Long folding tables, folding chairs, and a few couches are arranged in the room depending on the needs of the day.

Coffee Bill, a regular volunteer at most of the meals, already has finished brewing the coffee when I arrive for Spaghetti Lunch. He dispenses the coffee into pitchers for each table. Spaghetti has been served here every Tuesday for more than forty years. Two church members stir steaming pots of tomato and meat sauce and butter gigantic loaves of Italian bread. The large kitchen is crowded with equipment: an ancient gas stove and a huge steel island fill the center, and refrigerators, sinks, and counters cover every inch around the edges. There is room for six or eight people, but after I'm introduced to the three cooks, I'm sent away. Visitors are not allowed in the kitchen.

In the social hall, volunteers are busy with many tasks. Some set up the folding tables and chairs; others distribute pre-made bags of candy, placing one bag on each seat. Some volunteers pour milk into pitchers while others set the tables, adding plates, plastic flatware, napkins, a small bouquet of flowers, pitchers of milk and coffee, and salt and pepper shakers. A small crowd gathers outside the church, and occasionally someone comes in to ask if he or she can volunteer. The answer is no. Spaghetti Lunch is a traditional meal, meaning people from the church volunteer, and people who are food insecure eat. The one exception to this rule is Coffee Bill, who arrives early to make the coffee.

Once lunch is ready, a volunteer opens the outside door, and people move steadily up the stairs and find a seat. Those who have been waiting move quickly to get inside, but others wander in, a few at a time, leisurely visiting and chatting at several tables before taking a seat. Pastor Paula Green offers a quick prayer, and the volunteers serve a bowl of noodles covered with a thick meat sauce and a piece of garlic bread to each person. Some eat quickly and leave, and people who come in late easily find a free seat. The volunteers are intent on making sure every person gets a fair share of food, noticing if a coffee or milk pitcher is empty or if someone has not been served, checking back to be sure each person gets what he or she needs. One of the latecomers sits quietly at the end of my table, and I worry he won't get food, but the volunteers see him, quickly bring him food, and later a volunteer sits with him to chat. When the kitchen crew announces that seconds are available, many eaters bring their bowl to be refilled. After about forty-five minutes, 165 bowls of spaghetti have been served to about eighty people. When I leave, cleanup volunteers work around the few people who remain visiting at their tables.

LISTENING TO PEOPLE WHO ARE FOOD INSECURE

At first, St. James only offered Spaghetti Lunch. More than forty years ago, a church member, grateful for help the church provided her family when she was a child, decided to start a meal program. She developed the spaghetti sauce recipe, gathered a few volunteers, bought the supplies, and began serving thirty to thirty-five adults a week. Every week, Spaghetti Lunch features the same volunteers and the same recipe. The spaghetti is notably better than any other food program meat sauce I have ever had, with more meat and more flavor. From the start, the woman who began the meal program wanted to serve people in their seats to avoid asking persons to line up. Over the years the number of eaters has grown steadily.

Pastor Paula started coming to the Spaghetti Lunch six years ago in order to meet people. She sat down at the tables, was served a bowl of spaghetti, and began talking to the people who came to eat. First, she just got to know them. As she got to know them, she asked what they thought might be done differently. She asked again and again, "What do people need?" Someone from the neighborhood told Paula, "I have a kitchen, and I like to cook. But it's hard to get enough food on my disability check." The church is situated in the center of four subsidized housing high-rises, two of them restricted to adults with disabilities. Paula started the Food for All food pantry with that information and invited the people she met eating Spaghetti Lunch to be volunteers.

Coffee Bill told me his version of this story: "Larry got it started—Larry who passed away. It was Larry's idea to go to the food bank to get food for the food pantry. We were already feeding the people, and then Larry and Pastor Paula started Food for All. Then we got extra food from the food bank to use for Spaghetti Lunch and all the other programs." Eventually Paula invited other meal and recovery programs to use the church space the remaining days of the week, creating a church where food was available all the time.

When I visited, the Spaghetti Lunch volunteers had no intention of changing their style—food-secure church members volunteer, and people who are food insecure eat. As the church membership and leadership have changed to include many food-insecure people, that line seems arbitrary, but Paula lets it be. The food-insecure volunteers have learned the system and the rules: Anyone can volunteer for the food pantry, but only food-secure church members manage Spaghetti Lunch.

THE IMPORTANCE OF CREATING CONVERSATION

Coffee could be described as the great equalizer. At food ministries where I've volunteered and visited, everyone wants to know where it is, if it's hot, if it's good, and where the cream and sugar are. Coffee is the topic of conversation from the moment the doors open until the food is cleared away, and because of that, it's a great conversation starter. Conversation is the most important part of creating shared ministry. Before we can share ministry, we need to share our stories through ordinary conversation. If we really listen, our ordinary conversation can lead to an understanding and awareness of how other people live and of the forces that make some people's lives harder than others. When we allow ourselves to be moved by stories, we find ourselves in solidarity with people who live in poverty. And this feeling of solidarity makes us want to work with them to change the systems blocking their way forward. Small conversations make a big difference in our relationships.

Conversation between people with enough and people who are struggling helps us recognize our own privilege. The food-secure volunteers at a food ministry have the ability to set the hours of operation, to choose the location, to decide the menu and the method of serving, to make the rules and to enforce them. Even noticing circumstantial privileges helps us to notice the larger privileges in our lives, the power we have to get ahead and the power to live in a world governed by our own rules. We see that the systems that help some people hurt others. And the issues that may be mere annoyances for those of us with privilege can be catastrophic to those without. For example, I paid over $1,000 in fees for an unfair practice at my bank. They loaned me money to cover an overdraft and then collected interest on that money for years without telling me I had the loan. My bad money management made me angry at myself and at the bank. A man told me a story about his decision to spend $1,000 on Christmas gifts for his kids. A few months later, his wife lost her job. His poor money management made him homeless.

To hear stories like this and learn from them depends on creating space for conversation with people who are different from us—and we may have more in common with them than we think. When people share their stories with us, we ought to show them respect by taking their stories seriously, listening for their gifts, and asking what they need, knowing that they know more about what they need than we do. I hope every food ministry leader or volunteer will take the time to sit down with those who are food insecure; I hope we all take time to eat with, talk to, and listen to others. As we find God in one another, we come to understand the ways that we are called to create God's kingdom in the world.

HOW TO GET TO KNOW YOUR FOOD-INSECURE NEIGHBORS

Shared ministry starts with the people who need material resources. The first challenge is to find the people who are food insecure and learn from them about what they need. Paula ate at Spaghetti Lunch as a way to know people who were already hanging out in the church building. By spending most of their time building relationships, Paula and others from St. James let their food-insecure neighbors know that they could be trusted. They started with small talk, asking people how they were, how they dealt with the weather, if they rooted for a particular sports team; they didn't start by grilling people for information. Small talk is the grease that eases people into relationships.

Building relationships from small talk so that you can eventually ask the tough questions about what persons need and how the food ministry can serve them better takes time. Even if we attend a meal once a week and speak with a few people in attendance, months may pass before the conversation becomes anything but small talk. It was not uncommon for people who came to eat at Worcester Fellowship to hold back for six or eight months before sharing their story. Our aim is to have many people who trust us as conversation partners before we begin to ask for advice about the ministry. In my experience, first conversations often include people telling me that the meal program is great. They may mention how it helps them and how much they appreciate my work. In the beginning, people share what they think we want to hear. I remind myself that the systems for supporting people in poverty are set up in such a way that people who are the most compliant, who follow the rules, and who are grateful for what they are given get the most resources. As I mentioned in the previous chapter, I also find myself wanting to reward those who follow the rules. Until people get to know us and our ministries, many will be wary of being critical.

In the same way, as volunteers, we may start out awkward and fearful as we try to start conversations with strangers. We may be concerned that we don't know what to say or how best to say it. I've heard many workers lament that they just aren't good at small talk. In the end, I remind myself that food makes conversation easier and that taking the risk will be worth the initial discomfort. If we don't address our fears, we will never create relationships with persons who are different from us. Some great conversation starters include asking about the weather—"Do you think it will rain today?"—or about how the person's day has been. We can ask food-insecure persons ordinary questions that we would ask anyone else: "Where do you live?", "What do you do during the day?", and so on. People generally have chosen how they want to answer these questions and how much they want to share.

Building close connections to food-insecure people is also hard because their stories can be difficult. As we get to know people better, some of their stories may cause us to reexamine our own advantages or privileges in life. I remember sitting at a soup kitchen with a man who worked but did not get paid at a construction job in a neighboring town and suddenly realizing the work he did not get paid for may have been building a home in my newly constructed neighborhood. Conversations with people who have been hurt by our economic systems sometimes point out ways material assets come at a cost beyond what meets the eye.

Real listening does not involve judging the storyteller or the decisions he or she has made to handle life's challenges. As with any friend, the people we meet may not accept our advice and may continue to make what appear to be poor decisions. I've gotten to know people who have disappeared for months at a time and then reappeared without explanation. It is not our role to determine the next steps in their lives. The goal is only connection.

For church-based charities, our goal is more than providing food; our goal is demonstrating Christ's radical welcome, inviting others into the family of God. One of the most distinctive traits of Christianity is radical welcome—opening our arms to people on any faith journey. The relational work of the church is inviting people who are food insecure to be part of our church, part of our ministry, even leaders of our program. Galatians 3:28 reminds us "There is no longer Jew or Greek, there is no longer slave or free, there is no longer male and female; for all of you are one in Christ Jesus." Differences in race or ethnicity, class, or gender should not keep us separated from one another. We must overcome our fear and awkwardness in order to build up God's kingdom.

HOW TO GET STARTED IN RELATIONAL MINISTRY

For those who already lead or volunteer at a food ministry, the way toward relational ministry is to sit down at a meal and eat with the people and listen to their stories. At a food pantry, leaders and volunteers can stand in the line for food to start conversations. Some ministries set up a hospitality area for people to wait and visit before the food is ready for pickup. My cousin's church set aside a room for prayer and conversation during their food pantry and clothing giveaway events. One or more church members welcomed people in, asked what they needed, and listened to their stories. They then prayed together. They were surprised at the number of people who wanted someone to hear their prayer concerns. It provided a great opening to get to know people.

Whether we're attending another church's or community's program or the one in our own church building, I recommend joining in the meal or pantry in the same way that participants do. When I'm studying a ministry, I let the program director or manager know I'm there. When my goal is just to get to know people, I often simply join the line. At most food pantries, one must qualify to take food, so I just leave the line as I get close to the desk to check in. I don't pretend to be there to get food myself, and I'm honest if I'm asked why I'm there. I may share that I'm a member of a particular church or ministry that is interested in learning how to start a food program, or I may share that I'm interested in getting to know people in the community. If I'm visiting a food ministry where anyone is allowed to partake of the food, I will try to take smaller portions, but I don't visit without eating. Again, some of the easiest small talk is about the food itself! But by not eating, I would be making the point that I don't need the food, and that can be off-putting to those who do.

In Philadelphia, members of Trinity Memorial connected with the Welcome Church, an outdoor church reaching people who do not have homes. By attending the Welcome Church regularly, Trinity Memorial members got to know women who were cooking together. They invited them to use their building and then joined them for their monthly meal, creating their program Chat and Chew. Sara Miles, in *Take This Bread: A Radical Conversion*,[1] describes the people she met by standing in line, cooking, and simply visiting with the people who came to St. Gregory's food pantry in San Francisco. Miles learned that several shoppers were short-order cooks or wait staff, and others had experience in retail. These skills were needed to better organize the food pantry and to create a meal for the volunteers.

When the Reverend Mary Wolfe arrived as rector at Hope Evangelical Lutheran Church in Reading, Pennsylvania, the church ran Hope Pantry once a month. Some of the people who got food from the pantry were members of the congregation. As she got to know the church members, then the volunteers—some church members, some not—and later the people who came to shop for food, she heard the same story again and again: People wanted to eat together. Gathering volunteers from the church and the pantry, this church's meal, Hope's Table, was created by the people who needed food with people who wanted to provide food. Brighton Allston Congregational Church, affiliated with the United Church of Christ, located outside of Boston, Massachusetts, has a similar story of pantry shoppers and congregants wishing for a chance to eat together, and so the congregation invited shoppers to help them create a weekly meal.

WHAT I LEARNED ON THE STREETS

For those wanting to start a food ministry, the best way to meet people and learn about the needs of a community is to go where the people who need food congregate: at meals or food pantries, in shelters, on the streets, at warming-centers, in day-shelters, and on street corners. At Worcester Fellowship, my co-pastor and I did months of "street ministry" before holding the first worship service. (My mother told her friends I was a "street walker for Christ.") Street ministry is simply walking around in areas where people are hanging out, inviting people into conversation where they are. Here are some things we learned through our experiences.

Ask for Advice. Local service providers will know where to start your street walking. As you build relationships you can ask the people you meet where else you might go. I found people eager to share where I might meet more people—and also careful to advise me about more dangerous locations.

Travel in Pairs. Don't engage in street ministry alone (Jesus sent out the disciples two-by-two). However, large groups of volunteers can be intimidating to those you're trying to reach. A pair or trio of people is adequate. My co-pastor and I always did our street ministry during daylight hours to avoid being in the more dangerous areas of town at night.

Bring Items to Give Away. My co-pastor and I carried new white socks to hand out to those we saw on the street. We found that carrying a small gift (soft granola bars or sandwiches would also work) made starting conversations easier. At the beginning, our interactions were awkward. We couldn't tell who was food insecure just by looking at them, but we greeted people and asked them if they wanted socks. Note that desiring socks is common for people who are homeless, but food is better for identifying people who are food insecure.

But Don't Bring Too Much. Avoid giving away too much stuff. Identify what will help start conversations and don't bring more than that. You can't build a relationship when you hold the strings on material resources. If your church has a thrift shop, meal, or food pantry, certainly refer people to those resources or to those at other churches. At Worcester Fellowship, we didn't have financial resources, so we could honestly say, "What we have to offer is prayer." We also might add, "God loves you the way you are and wants you to have what you need." If you have the time, you can offer to go with someone to get resources. In any case, follow up the next time you see them. It will feel awkward to not meet every person's need—and that feeling gets worse as you get to know people better. But once you are the source of *stuff*, it will be more difficult to build a real relationship.

Find a Meal to Visit. Early on, one of the people we met suggested we visit the local Salvation Army; in Worcester they have meals every weekday. After that, my co-pastor and I walked our usual route and attended a meal at the Salvation Army each week. In terms of talking to people, I found the meal easier because it gave me the opportunity to ask questions: "Is this the right place to stand in line?", "Where is the coffee?", "Where do I put my dirty dishes?", and "Is the soup good?" Of course, eventually I knew the answers to those questions, but I still could ask, "Can I sit next to you?" as an icebreaker for further conversation.

Allow Time for Building Trust. Finding people and making small talk will take more time than you expect. At Worcester Fellowship we went out once a week for six weeks before we invited people to lunch and worship on Christmas Day—and no one came. It was several months later that we tried again on the following Easter. That time we had twelve people commit to doing a specific task and six of those people showed up.

Develop a Routine. Once you have identified good places to visit, make it a routine. It is best if the same people can visit almost every week. You want to get to the stage where you come in and people recognize that you belong in that space. As you get to know people, the conversations will change. Ask about how they are, and about things people told you about the week before. Some people like to bring a list of resources available, although I found that the people on the streets knew the details of those programs better than I did. It is helpful to know any new news about the shelters, food stamps, difficult landlords, and health service organizations.

Hold Stories in Confidence. Eventually someone will begin to tell you their story. Hold that story in confidence, telling only your supervisor for this work, and only if you need advice on how to handle a situation. Also hold the stories you are told lightly. Remember our system rewards people who tell good stories. Listen for the underlying feelings. Ask questions which don't doubt the story or require them to defend themselves, but rather get at how they feel, what they will do next, how can you hold them in prayer.

Offer Prayer. Prayer is a greater gift than those of us with plenty may understand. When asking people on the streets and at meals and pantries for prayer requests, you may be surprised at the underlying pain you discover in people's lives. I try to close all conversations with the question of whether there is anything I should be praying for them. Be sure to ask this question several minutes before you need to move on; sometimes this is where the real depth of the conversation will begin.

Check In on Fellow Volunteers. My co-pastor and I ended each session of street ministry by checking in with each other and with all the volunteers who had gone out with us. She and I shared information that could be helpful to our ministry, though we only shared an individual's specific story if we needed advice for next time. We both took the opportunity to name what had been hard in our conversations and relationship-building that day and to think through what we might do differently next time.

Meeting the people we wanted to serve and spending time listening to their stories was difficult, exhausting work, but it was work that got easier over time. As my co-pastor and I got to know the people in our community, they began introducing us to others, and we started to feel like we belonged. The key is to stick to it, even during the weeks when we feel like nothing significant is happening. Some people may never want to share their lives and stories with us, and that can be disappointing.

Many will appreciate the time we take to listen to them, to check in on them, and, ultimately, to create a relationship with them.

SOME PEOPLE DON'T WANT TO TALK

Soon, Alan was in charge of lunch at Worcester Fellowship. He was good at the things the paid leadership was not; however, he didn't want anyone telling him what to do. I was determined to get to know him, to offer him a listening ear. I wanted to be the person providing exactly the support he needed to move on to a better way of life.

"So how's it going, Alan?" I asked in the lull that occurs as the lunch line starts moving.

"It's good. I'm pretty sure we have enough lunches for everyone to have seconds," he replied.

"No, I mean with you. How are *you?* How is your life going right now?"

"Fine." He walked away.

One day the wind was blowing the snow sideways across the common, and I offered him a ride home. I imagined we might get a chance to talk.

"I like to walk," he said. "It builds up my body heat."

Another day, I tried a direct approach: "Tell me about your family."

"They are fine. Some things are just private."

After Alan told me about a guy he'd met who was new in town, I cautiously continued the conversation by asking, "What brought you to Worcester?"

Alan replied, "It seemed like a nice city. Will you give this lunch to Bob? I saved him one with tuna."

Alan wanted to be recognized as a leader—nothing more, nothing less.

DISCUSSION QUESTIONS

1. How will you get to know people who are food insecure in your community? Where will you go? Who would be interested in doing this work with you?

2. Is starting conversations with strangers difficult for you? Why or why not? In what ways can you improve your conversation skills?

3. Gather people interested in building relationships at your pantry or meal program and spend some time in pairs starting conversations with each other. One person can practice asking questions or starting small talk while the other person responds. Then, switch roles. Afterward, share what you learned in listening to each other.

PART TWO

LET THEM LEAD

FOUR

CULTURAL CONFLICT

The food pantry at St. James Church is a two-day affair that takes place on the third Wednesday and Thursday of each month. On Wednesday mornings, Pastor Paula picks up a couple of people from her neighborhood, drives to the food bank, selects food, and loads up the rented van. Andrea, the director of the pantry, orders the food ahead of time for the pantry and for several of the meals offered at the church. Paula and the volunteers choose additional items while at the food bank. When they arrive back at the church, volunteers meet the van to carry the food into the basement to store it out of the way. Early on Thursday mornings, forty-some volunteers, most of whom are food insecure, arrive to set up the food pantry. The volunteers divide the food by type—fresh vegetables, meat, grains, cereals, canned soups, and canned vegetables—and then set out the food on tables arranged around the room. In the sanctuary, cookies, candy, lemonade, and coffee create a hospitality station for people waiting—some for as long as three hours—for their turn to shop the pantry.

Before the pantry opens, the volunteers cook a meal and eat together, providing time for conversation and relationship-building among the volunteers as well as a time for announcements and celebrations related to the ministry. Additionally, the volunteers get to shop the pantry before it opens, and they either lock their bags of groceries in a storeroom or take them home to their nearby apartments. At 1:00 p.m., the pantry opens. By opening time, a line of more than two hundred people has formed. In an effort to discourage early morning waiting outside the church, each person receives a random number as he or she arrives—so being first in line does not guarantee being first to shop.

Despite the number system, many people continue to show up hours before starting time, waiting outside in the cold or heat. Paula hates keeping them outside but doesn't have a place inside for them to wait as the setup is being completed. One morning, she announced to the line, "The pantry doesn't open until one this afternoon, but if any of you want to come inside to volunteer, you are welcome to join us. I can't let people in except to volunteer." About thirty left the line and came inside. Most were elderly, and few spoke English. Did they understand that they had just volunteered? Perhaps not, but Paula found tasks for each of them. The result was chaos. Some people didn't understand the jobs they were given or Paula's directions, and some didn't understand they were volunteering at all. But Paula stuck with it and developed a cadre of an additional ten volunteers who came every week, some to staff distribution tables, some to distribute food among the tables, others to help with hospitality.

This work may be the most difficult part of St. James's ministry. Paula uses a translation app on her phone and the help of a volunteer translator and bilingual students in the community. Still, English-speaking volunteers continue to complain that these new volunteers are stealing food. The student volunteers refuse to translate anything that will correct or reprimand their elders. The language barrier is immense. Learning someone else's culture is hard work. Integrating volunteers from many different cultures is even harder. The churches I've visited are more diverse than most but still are primarily white. The food pantries and meals all serve multicultural populations. Integration is both a gift and a source of conflict. Like in the first-century church, breaking boundaries among persons of different cultures, ethnicities, and language is hard work. The issues that arise from language barriers are the most visible. The issues that arise from culture differences are more hidden.

The ministries I visited all used shared ministry to ease the conflicts surrounding language and culture. By working together on a specific task, people get to know one another and learn to work with the differences they bring to the chore. As the work is accomplished, the two or three begin to trust that the others in their team can and will do the work. At St. James, Paula makes sure that the persons standing in line know they can come in early if they are willing to volunteer, and many take advantage of that opportunity. At Brighton Allston Congregational, the pastor and volunteers intentionally invite eaters and shoppers from many cultures to come to worship or to volunteer. The Rev. Donna Maree in Philadelphia is intentional about inviting women of different races to cook and eat together at Trinity Memorial's Chat and Chew dinner. Some meal programs and pantries I visited sought out bilingual volunteers to ease the cultural tensions. By making sure people of all different races and ethnicities are explicitly welcomed, the ministries follow the first-century example of leadership. Each ministry makes a space where it is okay to talk about race, language, and ethnicity. They are intentional about doing outreach that acknowledges and affirms racial and ethnic difference. This makes it so volunteers can do the individual work to build relationships with one another while they work together to serve their neighbors.

CULTURAL CONFLICT IN THE EARLY CHURCH

What does the biblical witness tell us about how to negotiate cultural differences in our programs? The earliest Christian worship practices centered on shared meals as described in

Acts 2 and Acts 6. When large groups gathered for meals in the first century, the event typically included breaking bread, sharing wine, a meal, reading, prayer, and a symposium or discussion after the meal. This type of gathering was the first experience of church for this new faith.[1] The idea of only having a small piece of bread at Communion to symbolize a meal did not develop until much later. Additionally, first-century city housing in Jerusalem was organized around shared courtyards, which provided a space large enough for the new community to gather to eat in members' homes.[2] While it was unusual at that time for people to eat with anyone outside their social circle, Luke uses the word *believers* rather than *friends* in Acts 2:44 (NIV),[3] implying that this is a gathering of people from many different backgrounds. People are crossing the traditional boundaries of family and heritage. Because everyone has given up their possessions, everyone is poor, or perhaps everyone is rich.

In the following story in Acts 6, we see the first church-based meals program and, with it, cultural conflict:

During those days, when the disciples were increasing in number, the Hellenists complained against the Hebrews because their widows were being neglected in the daily distribution of food. And the twelve called together the whole community of the disciples and said, "It is not right that we should neglect the word of God in order to wait on tables. Therefore, friends, select from among yourselves seven men of good standing, full of the Spirit and of wisdom, whom we may appoint to this task, while we, for our part, will devote ourselves to prayer and to serving the word." What they said pleased the whole community, and they chose Stephen, a man full of faith and the Holy Spirit, together with Philip, Prochorus, Nicanor, Timon, Parmenas, and Nicolaus, a proselyte from Antioch. They had these men stand before the apostles, who prayed and laid their hands on them. The word of God continued to spread; the number of disciples increased greatly in Jerusalem, and a great many of the priests became obedient to the faith. (vv. 1-7)

As the community of new believers grows, welcoming new converts into the existing households becomes more difficult.[4] Acts 6:1 says, "The Hellenists complained against the Hebrews." This portion of Acts predates outreach to the Gentiles; all followers of Jesus are Jewish. The Hebrews are locals, from Jerusalem and Galilee, while Hellenists are Jews born and raised in other parts of the Roman Empire, part of the Jewish Diaspora. Hebrews offer the community meals in their homes, and the Hellenists are guests of these meals. Essentially, Hebrews are insiders while the Hellenists are outsiders, although they may have brought more sophisticated meal customs with them.[5]

The Hebrews would know Greek, the language of the Empire, but the Hellenists would not know Aramaic, the local language, and may not be included in decision-making. The Hellenists may not be as orthodox in their religious practices as the Hebrews. The insider Hebrews have set up the structures and rules for these shared meals, leaving the outsider Hellenists disenfranchised.[6] The solution to the conflict is blessing or ordaining seven Hellenistic (men) to lead the meal program. The apostles listen to the voices of the outsiders and make space for leadership alongside the existing structures. For today's food ministries, this suggests that churches must make leadership positions available for today's outsiders—people who are food insecure.

SERVING AND BEING SERVED

Most scholarship presumes that the point of Acts 6:1-7 is to introduce Stephen and others at the conclusion of the story. Scholars often see this passage as a setup for Stephen's martyrdom in the next chapter. This viewpoint keeps scholars from asking questions about the widows—who are they and how are they being neglected?

These widows could be among the women who are funding the church, like the women mentioned in Luke 8:1-3 who funded Jesus' ministry. Luke doesn't specify that they are widows, but it is likely, as it would be the husbands described as the providers if they were present. It is easy to jump to the conclusion that the widows are the poorest of women. There are many poor widows in the bible, most often described as "widows and orphans," but widows of wealthy men are not likely to be poor. The text does not say or imply poverty. Earlier, in Acts 2:44, we learn that the believers are holding "all things in common." No one is poor, and no one is rich after joining the community of believers. Acts 4:34 assures us "there was not a needy person among them."

Additionally, the early church had a group of leaders called "widows," likely a subset of women who had lost husbands, dedicated to the work of prayer as seen in 1 Timothy 5:3-16.[7] The "saints and widows" called to witness to Tabitha/Dorcas' resurrection in Acts 9:41 are considered by scholars to be a specific order of believers, like the later orders of deacons and priests.[8] It is possible the widows are set apart leaders of the community.

If the Hellenists' complaint that their widows are "being neglected in the daily distribution of food" (v. 1) is not about charity, what, then, is it about? We know from Acts 2:46 that the community is eating together every day. In the commentary "The Acts of the Apostles: Introduction, Commentary, and Reflections" in *The New Interpreter's Bible*, Robert W. Wall notes that the Greek *diakonia* is interpreted as *distribution* in Acts 6:1, but in verse 4, it is translated *ministry of the word* in the NIV or *serving the word* in the NRSV.[9] The English *distribution* gives the impression of something handed out, while *ministry* or *serving* could have to do with the daily meal. Being neglected or overlooked in the daily *diakonia* could mean the widows didn't get a turn to serve or didn't get a turn to eat.[10]

While the majority of scholarship leans toward the widows not getting a turn to eat, that idea rests on the presumption that this is a charitable distribution to poor widows, which as we have seen, is not the case. This interpretation requires that women who are attending meals along with the other believers are not getting enough food or are not getting food at all. While it is possible that people are starving the widows in their community, I find the other possibility more likely.

The complaint could be that the widows were overlooked in the *ministry at the table* or are neglected in the opportunity for *serving at table*. The New Testament scholar Elisabeth Schüssler Fiorenza argues that Luke prioritizes the ministry of the word (preaching) over the ministry of the table (Eucharist)—thus the twelve in verse 2 don't want to be distracted from preaching in order to oversee the table. She translates the "distribution of food" as "serving at table," that is the preparing, serving, and cleaning up after the community dinner or Eucharist celebration.[11] *Diakonia,* where we get our word *deacon,* is about caring for others. Women in this time often cared for others by organizing meals, as we see with Martha and Mary in Luke 10:38-42. My preferred interpretation is that the Hellenistic widows were not getting their turn to serve the meal.

PEOPLE WANT TO SERVE

I relish those times when I go home after a long day of volunteering and I think to myself, *That was wonderful. I think I got more out of this than the people who came to eat!* On those days, I feel satisfied, proud, and exhausted, but more than anything I am reminded of the meaning of my work. They remind me of the Holy Spirit's presence in my life and ministry. Sometimes these good days include someone thanking me for my work in a heartfelt way. Sometimes I am filled with gratitude for the opportunity to sit with someone as he or she shares his or her story. Other times, I connect with another volunteer on a different level and feel the gift of shared service. These moments make the whole experience feel worth it.

For me, these unexplainable encounters with God and with others are church. I've talked to other volunteers and organizers at food ministries throughout the United States, and they speak of their holy encounters in the same way. They all agree that what they do feels like so much more than work. They all sense that there is more going on than offering people food to nourish their bodies. Food ministry feels like a higher calling—and it is. God calls us to this work. And for this reason, I believe that we can do our work in better ways than we are now.

Though the feeling of community, purpose, and meaning that develops between volunteers is real, the eaters are not invited into that feeling in direct-service ministries. So often those who are food secure work together to build a food ministry, but they don't welcome people who are food insecure into their work or into their churches. Because we have a narrow view of who is a leader and who is a volunteer, we don't recognize the many potential volunteers around us.

Every community has more leaders than it realizes. Leadership is not a limited resource. When we see leaders in persons who had originally been recipients of our ministries, we create shared ministry, which presumes that all people—those with and without access to sufficient food resources—want to serve others. A first step in creating shared ministry involves those of us in power giving up some of that power in order to include those who have previously been left out. While many food ministries feel like community because they include sitting and eating with people in need, asking about their lives, and treating them with respect, these communities remain divided as long as rules require that only some people can serve and only some people can eat. When we include more people in our ministries as leaders and volunteers, we contribute to their sense of belonging. Additionally, working together broadens the definition of hospitality: People are welcomed not only as outsiders and guests but also as members of the community.

People should be seen (by themselves and by others) as gifted and be given the opportunity to work using their gifts. There is dignity in work that gives us control and authority and the ability to help others. Direct-service charities must make space for people who need resources to find a place to work. We need to recognize individuals' gifts and to see leadership abilities. It is in using their gifts that a person is welcomed as an equal into community.

This is not about requiring people to work. Volunteering should not be required as payment for the resources provided. Instead, this is about looking for gifts in each person and focusing on gifts more than needs. We can trust that God is in the world—not only in the church—and look for God's presence in each person we meet. We can invite people to share their gifts with us. Shared ministry makes space for voluntary involvement in work that is meaningful and uses the skills that people bring with them, whether they come with material resources or not.

A test of our equality is to ask if new volunteers have the power to change our food ministry. If they make suggestions, do we try out their ideas? Can we give away some authority for determining how the program is organized? Do we allow our relationships with volunteers to change us? At the same time, the goal is to welcome people without the presumption that they need to be changed or fixed or to be like us in order join us. We must imagine the people coming to eat are *part* of our church, rather than simply visitors.

Recognizing new gifts leads to a more diverse community and to more of a sense of belonging. While to be a guest is more pleasant than being a client, to be invited to be a leader is an invitation to truly be one of us. Without the rights of leadership, the people who come to receive food are not given the full rights of membership into the community. Shared ministry intentionally expands the rights of leadership to people with and without food security.

We see from the story in Acts and from the experiences of churches engaged in shared ministry that more people can be involved in leadership. In Acts, Stephen, named a leader in response to conflict, later becomes a leader in the church. The people at St. James who didn't speak English became faithful volunteers. At many ministries, it took a conscious effort by the leadership to be sure the volunteers crossed cultural barriers. This required getting to know people whose first language was not English or interacting with people of different races. By working together and listening to one another, we can be part of overcoming cultural conflicts in our ministries.

DISCUSSION QUESTIONS

1. What stands out to you about the story of the widows in Acts 6? What does it tell you about ministry?

2. Name the cultural conflicts in your local community. How does the culture of your church reflect the culture of the neighborhood in which the church resides?

3. How do you balance giving and receiving in your own life? How can you encourage and empower others to be both givers and receivers in your food ministry?

FIVE

EVERYONE CAN VOLUNTEER

I n each box, there's a container of shelf-stable milk. Take it out, and put in a gallon of fresh milk instead," David Husselbee explains.

The college student listening to the directions looks confused. "Shelf-stable . . . ?"

David reaches into the box and pulls out the cardboard milk container. "It's shelf-stable milk, meaning it doesn't have to be refrigerated. We have fresh milk, so we'll save the boxed milk for another day." He pulls out the container and sets it on the cart. The student follows his lead and removes the milk from each box and then heads to the back cooler to fill the cart with fresh milk to put out for the shoppers.

It's 9:15 a.m. on Saturday, at the Brighton Allston Congregational Church food pantry, which opens at 10:00. The place is bustling with volunteers. In the basement, David directs volunteers as they load up boxes of food for shoppers. Yesterday a crew of high school students filled boxes with nonperishable foods. This morning, frozen meats, fresh fruits and vegetables, a gallon of milk, and a dozen eggs are added to each box.

Kathleen Babbin sits at the back door of the church with a stack of laminated numbers. She greets people with a smile as they come in and sends them to the right into the sanctuary to wait for their turn to shop. A few tell Kathleen they want to visit the thrift shop or to volunteer, and she sends them to the left into the fellowship hall.

While I am chatting with Kathleen, a woman wobbles tentatively out of the sanctuary. "I lost my number," the woman announces.

"Where is your husband?" Kathleen asks.

"Is he here?"

"Yes, you came in with your husband."

"Oh, I'll look for him." The woman heads into the fellowship hall, and a few minutes later she reappears with her husband.

He holds up their number, saying, "We have one," and takes his wife's arm.

"That's great. Just sit together in the sanctuary, and they'll call your number." Kathleen turns back to me. "We switched the setup to have people wait in the sanctuary."

Kathleen is a middle-aged white woman with red hair and a quick smile. She is a deacon and has been a church member at Brighton Allston for four years. I ask her why she volunteers.

"I was coming to community supper, and Pastor Karen asked me to come to worship in a non-pushy way. It was a rainy day, just like this. My outdoor plans were canceled so I came here. They had me at hello." Six months later, the church invited Kathleen to become a deacon.

Another deacon on the opposite side of the sanctuary calls out numbers and instructs people to wait in the doorway for their turn to sign in. The wait is about half an hour. Sister Maggie Kilduff of the Religious of the Sacred Heart and another woman check people in while the church administrator looks over their shoulders to help with the iPad sign-in system. Two or three volunteers are moving around the thrift store, and a visiting pastor sits ready to help with whatever is needed. Each person needs to be found on the list or entered as new; then, each person must sign that he or she qualifies for the pantry. A short white woman in slacks and a sweater, Sister Maggie explains to me that she is sure she can learn the new technology, but it is new. "The printed list was so easy. You just found their name and had them sign that." The administrator is apologetic as he explains that the iPad may slow down registration, but it takes hours off the reporting end. Sister Maggie assures him she is fine with it.

Sister Maggie was at a local parade when she met Pastor Karen Fritz and one of the Brighton Allston deacons and found out they needed volunteers. "It was all uphill from there," Sister Maggie laughs. "God only knows why I keep coming back." She calls over to the church administrator. "We can't find this woman on the list, and she is here every time. I don't know how else to look."

"Try searching for her street address."

Sister Maggie turns back to the woman waiting her turn to pick up groceries. "I'm sorry. We are just learning how to do this. You are very patient with us!" Eventually, the address appears, the woman signs the screen, and Sister Maggie gives her a sticky note that mentions she has one child. Sister Maggie turns back to me. "Of course, this is why I come back. For the volunteers, for the people I meet, in order to see Jesus here waiting his turn for food. They don't want to have to ask for food, you know, so if I can offer a smile, it's worth it."

Once checked in, the shopper proceeds down the wide, steep stairs to the basement social hall, which contains ten tables. On each table are two boxes of food and a stack of plastic bags. Karen Essrow, a volunteer from the local community, greets the shopper, hollers out the number of children, and helps the shopper choose a table to sort through a box. "Each box is mostly the same, but you can poke a bit and pick the one you want." The woman asks about the different packages of bread, and Karen trades away her loaf of sliced rye for a bag of day-old bagels. The shopper checks the label on each can and box as she chooses which items to slip into plastic bags and into her rolling cart. Another volunteer brings out the additional "children's box" with materials specifically for families with children—more milk, a bottle of juice, and single-serving applesauce snacks. Two other shoppers choose items from their boxes.

Karen found this pantry by searching online, and she chose it as a place to volunteer because it had no restrictions on timing. "I wanted a place I could come when I wanted to and miss when I was busy." I ask if that has worked out for her, and she laughs. "Well, actually, I love it here, and I adjust my schedule so I don't miss it."

"Do you feel connected to the church?"

"I'm Jewish. I feel connected to the people who come here." Karen says she's noticed that some of the volunteers also are food pantry recipients, and she likes that. "This place is small enough that you can actually get to know the other volunteers and get to know the people coming for food. It's a friendly place."

A student from the local college brings out another children's box and helps the shoppers pack their items onto a rolling cart. He and a group of others are doing community service hours, assigned by the college when they had an unauthorized party. The students aren't shy about telling everyone that they think the forty-hour punishment is unfair. This is their third visit. I ask the student how his feelings about the punishment affect the work he does. "Does it make you hate doing this?"

"Oh, no, I love this place. Everyone is helpful, and it's great to help people." He calls over a friend, and they lift the rolling cart up the stairs, down the hall, and back down the outside stairs, the shopper following along, chatting and thanking them.

The downstairs distribution center has more volunteers than shoppers. Two high school kids in the back room are packaging extra boxes of food for when the first batch runs out. A man sits by the cooler, reading a newspaper but at the ready to bring out more milk, eggs, and frozen turkey when needed. Two people add bread, fruits, and vegetables to the extra boxes and carry them down to distribution tables, returning with items that shoppers have left behind to be re-shelved. Other volunteers chat with shoppers, making sure they are getting what they need, asking how they are, wondering if the rain will stop this afternoon.

Ladouceur Marie Lourdy asks a couple of the students to carry her baby stroller down the stairs and hands four-month-old Dylan to other volunteers so she can assist the shoppers. She came to Brighton from Haiti just six months ago and loves to volunteer. She heard about the pantry from another volunteer at the nearby diaper ministry. "I do it for the smiles," she tells me. "It feels like I'm really doing something to help."

David Husselbee, who explained the shelf-stable milk to the young volunteer, is a young white man with muscled arms and a quiet smile. He has been volunteering for several years and is a leader—guiding volunteers to new tasks, answering questions, redirecting people, finding more tasks—but insists he is not in charge. I ask how he found this pantry.

"Well, I was assigned it as community service."

"Oh, like the other college kids here today?"

David laughs. "No, like an actual crime. I had to do it as part of a trial proceedings."

"How much time did you have to do?"

"Four months."

"So why are you still here?"

"I like that it's not professional. The volunteers matter. And everyone was super nice to me. They cared."

"And then you ended up in charge?" I ask.

"I'm not really in charge, but I know a lot about what is going on here. I took on more responsibilities as I knew more about it. Some days, there are not many people, and we can run the program with hardly any volunteers. Other weeks, we find jobs for lots of volunteers. And when there are new people, I help them find their place."

"Did doing your community service here make a difference in your life?"

"Oh, yeah. Now I have a full-time job at a local hospital, and on the weekends, I do this. It keeps me out of trouble."

"What would you tell people who want to create a pantry like this?"

"It's totally doable. The groceries come from the food bank and from food recovery programs. It costs just $150 each time we do it. We work with lots of volunteers or just a few. Working with the basement stairs is the hardest part of it."

The pantry closes at 1:00 p.m., and the volunteers are done by 1:30 p.m., after saving the shopper data on the iPad and re-shelving the remaining nonperishable items. The downstairs tables are cleaned off to be ready for Wednesday's dinner, and the sanctuary and fellowship hall are ready for church the next day.

DIFFERENT FORMS OF SHARED MINISTRY

Brighton Allston Congregational Church uses shared ministry for all of its programs, integrating volunteers from all walks of life into its ministries. The church has a paid pastor, a part-time administrator, and large numbers of volunteers. Most of the volunteers aren't connected to the church, but many are members and some are deacons. Even more volunteers—church members and not, food secure and not—attend the weekly Wednesday meal. Similarly, Sunday worship and the Sunday and Wednesday Bible studies also are filled with a mix of members and non-members each week. It is hard to tell who is food secure and who is not. Brighton Allston's model for shared ministry is just one method, and after visiting several shared-ministry programs, I've identified four ways of engaging food-insecure volunteers.

First, some churches use mostly food-secure volunteers but have places to include a few food-insecure volunteers. Second, some divide the work by task. For example, food-secure people cook, and food-insecure people set up, serve, or clean up. A third model includes a few food-secure people in leadership roles while most of the volunteers are food insecure. A fourth model—like that employed at Brighton Allston—combines the previous three strategies such that there is no delineation between who is food secure and who is food insecure.

MOSTLY FOOD-SECURE VOLUNTEERS

The Downtown Welcome Table is at Haywood Street Congregation in Asheville, North Carolina, a United Methodist Church. Open Table is the meal at UrbanMission in Pomona, California, affiliated with the United Church of Christ and the Christian Church (Disciples of Christ). At both churches, most of the meal volunteers are food secure. They employ shared ministry by allowing and encouraging people who are food insecure to volunteer. Both churches began their ministries by asking people who needed food what they wanted and by developing their programs around what they heard.

Emily Bentley Pettigrew was Haywood Street's full-time, paid "Companion Coordinator" when I visited. The word *companion* replaces *volunteer* in order to emphasize walking with people rather than doing for people. She coordinated companions for two meals, serving close to 700 people each week, plus a number of other ministries. The church has several other full-time paid positions, including a pastor and a banquet steward. It is not a food-secure congregation doing outreach to a food-insecure and homeless community; it is diverse congregation sharing food and services with its community. The church's Christian identity is central to its outreach with people who don't have homes or sufficient food.

Companions are trained to avoid thinking about fixing people and to approach the companioning experience as an opportunity to learn to love their neighbor and community. The monthly orientation for potential companions sets the tone by starting in the sanctuary and focusing more on the church's theology of welcome than on how to run the dishwasher. Those leading the orientation encourage using people's names, asking people how they are, and finding out where people are from and what brought them there.

Emily guesses about 20 percent of Haywood's volunteers are food insecure, although the church doesn't ask or keep records of that information. Some are homeless; more are marginally housed or have been homeless in the past. "[The food-insecure companions] are here the earliest and stay the longest and are the most consistent companions," Emily explains. "I think they realize more than any of us that we have to share our resources and help out one another. They've had to share resources, and they understand the importance more than our more privileged companions. A lot of people have the opinion that poor folk can't give back and don't want to, but that isn't true."

The environment at the Downtown Welcome Table is intended to attract companions who might be uncomfortable volunteering. The church emphasizes the importance of participation more than efficiency, and the church will find volunteer opportunities in the ministry for anyone with any skill level. If they have three volunteers setting the tables, then why not ask one to do forks, one knives, and one spoons? Why not ask two people to push a cart across the room? Additionally, Haywood has enough space to offer a separate waiting room for persons to drink coffee and eat snacks before the meal opens, meaning persons can come inside and potentially take on the role of companioning others while waiting for the meal.

Food-secure volunteers have a more difficult time understanding the culture of Haywood Street Congregation. Emily says, "The idea of *being with* instead of *doing for* goes against the culture." It is her job to reinforce this attitude again and again. She checks in with every volunteer, redirects people as necessary, and pulls everyone together to "circle up" before each meal. She uses the time to remind people the goal is community, not just service. Helping visiting groups that come once or twice a year understand the culture is a different challenge, but Emily tries to be as accommodating as possible. She has found some young people—especially those from privileged backgrounds—feel uncomfortable in working alongside those who are less fortunate, but Emily insists that discomfort is a valuable challenge. Often Haywood Street meshes the ideas of *being with* and *doing for* by encouraging first-time groups to come and eat and stay for cleanup. This encourages the food-secure volunteers to spend time *being with* before they start the expected *doing for* aspect of volunteering. Even staff persons who try to teach the culture to others have to pull themselves back to *being with* over and over again. "It's simple work, but it's not easy," Emily explains.

UrbanMission in Pomona, California, encounters similar challenges—the simplicity and difficulty of the work—yet defining moments emerge from the gathering of diverse people sharing with one another. Both Haywood Street and UrbanMission consider their congregation to be all the people who come into their space, rather than restricting it to worship attendance. UrbanMission's structure, however, is quite different from Haywood's. Other than one full-time paid pastor, everyone else—including two ordained pastors and a meals director—are unpaid volunteers. I visited on a Sunday when the volunteer cooks are members of a Chinese-American church and again when a diverse assembly of local nursing students made dinner. Stephen Yorba Patten, the volunteer Community Wellness Minister, oversees the pantry, meal, garden, and health center. He is a white Disciples of Christ minister with a lengthy association to city of Pomona. He uses his connections to recruit individuals and organizations, including a large youth contingent from the high school where he teaches.

While waiting for dinner, I notice that a couple of the volunteers have also come to eat. While it's not required, many who come to eat do a little to help with the meal. A few parents watch the kids in the courtyard, someone takes out the trash, another shows up early to weed the garden. When one volunteer realizes the food pantry is open a bit earlier than usual, he directs those waiting for the meal to take advantage of the pantry as well. Many who come early to eat help with set-up; almost everyone clears their own place and helps fold and stack the chairs. All the people who come to serve take a break to sit and eat the meal set out on two long lines of tables, with fifteen people on each side.

VOLUNTEERS DIVIDED BY TASKS

Monday Lunch at The Cathedral Church of St. Paul (Episcopal) in Boston, Massachusetts, is a ministry of Many Angels Needed Now and Always (MANNA), a leadership development organization for people who are homeless and at risk of homelessness. MANNA provides music, writing, meditation, and recovery ministries to the Boston community in addition to Monday Lunch and Eucharist.

Monday Lunch employs clear lines of responsibility: Indoor suburban churches provide lunch four Mondays a month. Church members do all the cooking—some at their home church and some at the cathedral—and they clean their own cooking equipment. They stand behind a serving table and fill plates and bowls and carry trays of dessert and fruit to each table. Some groups also make bagged dinners for eaters to take with them as they leave. On fifth Mondays, a group of MANNA leaders cooks the meal.

No matter who is cooking, those who eat come to the fellowship hall and sit at round tables with flatware, napkins, and flowers in vases set by MANNA members—people who are homeless and marginally housed. The MANNA team staffs coffee and juice stations and, after prayers and announcements, picks up plates of food from the serving table and carries them to each table of eaters. Servers listen to special dietary requests—no meat, no salad, less of this, more of that—and work with the cooks to address them. Someone from MANNA directs the servers going around the room, making sure no table or eater is missed. After being served in their seats, eaters go up to the serving table for seconds. MANNA volunteers begin clearing the spaces of people who have left. These food-insecure volunteers clean tables, fold chairs, store supplies for next time, empty the trash, and set up for the Monday Eucharist.

Some of the indoor church members move out from behind the serving table to sit and visit with those who are eating. Some prefer to keep to the kitchen and behind the serving table, limiting their visiting to questions about the food served. The separation of duties provides some control of the meal service and makes space for food-insecure volunteers while allowing the food-secure people an opportunity to engage according to their comfort level. Worcester Fellowship also uses the divided-work model, with churches that have buildings providing lunch each week and the responsibilities for handing out the lunch divided evenly between the food-secure visiting congregation and food-insecure Worcester Fellowship members.

MOSTLY FOOD-INSECURE VOLUNTEERS

St. James has many ministries, but the Food for All pantry is distinctive in how it welcomes and depends upon volunteers who are almost all food insecure. Chat and Chew, the shared women's meal at Trinity Memorial Church in Philadelphia, Pennsylvania, is an interesting example of people who are food insecure cooking a meal for themselves once a month.

St. James has a full-time pastor who oversees the food ministries and building rental by other programs and a paid part-time pantry director who is food insecure. Some food-secure volunteers help with picking up the food at the food bank, but most of the remaining volunteers are food insecure. Pastor

Paula ensures there is someone who is food secure on the hospitality team handing out snacks as people wait their turn to shop. Staff from the food bank attend to demonstrate cooking strategies for healthy foods, and two people who are food secure check whether shoppers qualify for the food. I later discovered that the man breaking down recycling boxes for hours on end was also food secure. Beyond those few, forty or more volunteers are food insecure, many from the nearby subsidized housing high-rises. They carry food from the delivery cars and vans into the pantry, sort it, organize it by table, and sit behind the tables for distribution. Recently Paula found a way for people who are food insecure to do the food pick-up. From day one they have done the cleanup after the pantry closes and prepared a noontime meal for the other volunteers setting up for the pantry.

Chat and Chew is a monthly meal that is planned, cooked, eaten, and cleaned up by twelve women who don't have homes. Pastors from Trinity Memorial Church and the Welcome Church purchase the food. The women are given personal invitations to take part, and the core group remains the same from month to month. Because Trinity's kitchen is narrow and crowded, the group splits up from the beginning: half in the kitchen, cooking the meal, and half in the dining area, making sweet tea and coffee and setting the table and serving buffet. A few of the women take charge of particular parts of the meal—one making sure dessert is started early enough to be cooled for that night's dinner, another demonstrating what size to cut potatoes, a third checking that knives, forks, spoons, and napkins are in their proper places. The women who cook and eat together feel a sense of community in working together.

INTEGRATION OF FOOD-SECURE AND -INSECURE VOLUNTEERS

At Brighton Allston Congregational Church in Brighton, Massachusetts, and at Hope Lutheran Church in Reading, Pennsylvania, the church members themselves are a mix of food-secure and food-insecure people. The churches' ministries—both have a food pantry and a meal—reach out to their local communities and bring in volunteers, both food secure and food insecure, from beyond the congregations' members. Unlike the example where specific groups have designated tasks, at these churches everyone does everything based on interest and skill. Because so many members of these churches are food insecure or don't have homes, an outsider can't tell who fits into what food-security category. Both churches welcome outside groups to join them. Brighton Allston's visiting groups serve food to people seated at tables; Hope Lutheran sometimes asks visiting churches or community groups to provide food for its buffet line. The cook at Brighton Allston is food insecure; the one at Hope grew up using food pantries. When visitors cook for Hope, some of their food-insecure volunteers guide the visitors.

At Brighton Allston Congregational, volunteers lead the twice-monthly food pantry, the weekly meal, the secondhand shop, and the emergency cold-weather housing. The pastor often picks up the food from the food bank because so few of the pantry leaders and volunteers drive. Most of the leaders of the pantry are food insecure, but many food-secure members of the church come and visit with their neighbors as they shop. Some people come to the church's Wednesday dinner because they don't have food at home; others come to grab a meal between work and the evening Bible study. A mix of church members and visitors with disabilities stack plates and organize dirty dishes. People on parole work with college students to plate the food and carry it out to the seated diners. The coffee station is run by church members who pull in neighbors who came to eat to help them. Several of the people who appeared to be "just" eaters the night I visited the meal later came on Saturday to volunteer at the food pantry.

Hope Lutheran has a full-time pastor and a part-time secretary. Tuesday evening worship follows their meal. The evening I visited, a couple living in their car came in and offered to make coffee during prep, and the kitchen volunteers didn't pause but simply showed them where to find the supplies. Their food pantry check-in on Tuesdays is done by a church member, probably food secure, and the line is kept in order by a food-secure neighbor. Those behind the distribution tables are a mix of people from the neighborhood and from the church; at least half took a turn shopping the food pantry before the meal began.

START WHERE THE PEOPLE ARE

There are as many ways to engage in shared ministry as there are churches and faith communities. In my research, I expected to find that the churches I visited had started small in integrating shared ministry, perhaps by initially asking eaters to take on cleanup after the meal. In reality, many of these ministries decided to open all volunteer activities to everyone from the beginning. Churches that employed outside groups to bring food before they began shared ministry have worked out ways to combine the two systems of volunteering. All of the shared-ministry churches prioritized building relationships over any other criteria for their programs. Many of those church members emphasized that their Christian faith was essential in deciding how to organize their ministry. All of them found people who were qualified for leadership roles by getting to know them and then offering those roles to the people who had the skills necessary. None of the programs placed a high priority on training; instead, they spent their time *noticing* existing skills.

All of these shared-ministry programs have a few food-secure people in supervisory roles, but many of those leaders have a history of homelessness or food insecurity. There were many more volunteers in the shared-ministry sites than in the direct-service programs I visited in the same cities. Shared ministry prioritizes participation over efficiency. At all of these programs, volunteers described an overwhelmingly positive experience; they felt recognized, appreciated, and welcomed.

WHAT MAKES SHARED MINISTRY WORK?

While I was visiting with Rev. Mary Wolfe at Hope Lutheran Church in Reading, Pennsylvania, one of the parishioners who was scheduled to provide the evening meal for a youth program was sick. Mary mentioned this on Sunday, Monday, and Tuesday, each time commenting that we might need to figure out who would provide the meal on Wednesday. But she never made a plan for how it would happen. By Wednesday, when I joined Mary for lunch, there was still no clarity on who would provide the meal that night. I felt myself getting tense at the uncertainty of the situation, but Mary seemed unfazed. While Mary and I were eating, the sick parishioner called to report that she was better but not 100 percent, so she would order pizza for the meal. Mary thanked her profusely and turned back to me. I had to ask how she had remained so calm while not knowing what was going to happen.

"Well, she has a passion for this youth program. I guess I just believed she'd come through with an idea."

"Mary, you say this about everyone here—Dee has a gift, Karen has a passion, Will and Brenda and Margaret have gifts. What are you doing that makes all these people so willing and glad to volunteer?"

"This is a great congregation. I don't think it's . . ."

I cut her off. "Yes, you have great people, but I do think that you are doing something that makes this a place that people want to commit to, a place where people want to carry a project through to completion. I've been to a lot of churches that have someone who keeps everyone else out of the kitchen or someone who complains about new ideas and change. I think you are doing something that makes space for these volunteers. What is it?"

Mary thought a moment and answered slowly. "Maybe it's what I'm not doing." I waited for her to explain. "I don't rescue things. If people say something is broken and needs to be fixed—whether the building or a program—I wait for them to fix it or to find someone to fix it. The bulletin has a lot of typos, and I don't redo it. When we needed to provide food for the after-school program, I just mentioned that it needed to be done. I have never made dinner."

"So that makes space for people to step up?"

"Yes. Additionally, I'm realizing the importance of not redoing other people's work. If someone volunteers for a task and doesn't do it perfectly, then I accept it the way it is. People who want to volunteer can because there is no expectation of perfection."

"So their work will be accepted as it is?"

She paused and then nodded. "Really, it's more than that. I write thank-you notes. I look for whatever a person is doing, and I send them emails or handwritten cards or pull them aside and say thank you."

"Gratitude," I nod, understanding.

"I want to communicate that we are all in this ministry together. It's not *my* ministry; it's *our* ministry.

Mary's story matches what I saw in different ways at all of the churches I visited. Making space for people to do their best, accepting what people offer as volunteers, and being grateful for what gets done builds a strong team of volunteers. When we restrict the opportunities for volunteering, we limit the potential of our ministries. But when our volunteers feel appreciated, they will learn to do the ministry well, often bringing in additional volunteers and new energy for our programs.

HOW TO INCLUDE PEOPLE AS VOLUNTEERS

There is no "right way" to include food-insecure people in ministry. But as we get to know those persons who are food insecure and begin to build relationships with them, we also will get to know those persons' skills. What happens next is largely a function of the people we meet in our communities. At Worcester Fellowship, Alan found us, and we had to learn to move over and make space for him, while also respecting his skills and seeing him as an equal in the work. The goal isn't to establish a specific shared-ministry model but rather to let the relationships guide our planning. Even if we begin by employing one model for shared ministry, we can allow our programs to adapt and adjust depending on the needs and desires of the people we serve.

Some food ministries may find new leaders for their programs in persons who are food insecure. They may even decide to create a leadership team of food-insecure volunteers. Other food ministries may find someone with a specific set of skills that could be useful, and so they ask that person to help out. For those ministries who haven't identified food-insecure leaders yet can start by inviting food-insecure volunteers to help with setup and cleanup. When we ask for help, we will draw volunteers, but we must know and communicate precisely what we want and need. Details matter. Are there different table coverings available for different shaped or sized tables? Does the flatware go on the table or in the buffet line? Are tablecloths washed and used again or thrown away? Are just the tables wiped down or chairs too? Can volunteers help with dishwashing, or is the kitchen off-limits? We must be clear in our requests. If someone is doing something other than what we hoped for, we must decide quickly if it's okay and redirect them if it's not. It's easier to enforce rules that are clear from the start, but we must remember that our food-insecure volunteers may know more than we do. I'll never forget when someone helping with cleanup at a meal took the mop from me and demonstrated how to ensure the mop touched every part of the floor, then handed it back to me and left. He clearly knew more about mopping than I did.

For ministries that serve food, all volunteers, whether food secure or not, should follow ServSafe food-handling rules. ServSafe offers an online course that organizers of a food ministry can take. All volunteers are not required to take the course, but the kitchen supervisor should direct everyone to follow the rules. Public health regulations stipulate that people who work in the kitchen must wash their hands, wear gloves, and keep their hair away from their face and out of the food. Volunteers, whether food secure or insecure, will understand that there are health requirements for serving food. People who have worked as short-order cooks, dishwashers, and servers may already know these rules, perhaps better than the lawyers and pastors in the kitchen.

Many programs let eaters come inside early if they will help with setup. For the food ministries that practice this, make sure to have some food available—coffee, juice, or a snack. A volunteer can even help set up a hospitality table for the other volunteers. If possible, provide a locked or supervised space for volunteers' belongings. Otherwise people may feel compelled to carry their bags and other items as they volunteer. Yes, the wealthier volunteers may worry about their credit cards or cash, but we must remember that the poorer volunteers may be carrying everything they own. People need a way to protect their belongings.

We must trust that we will encounter some chaos along the way, but perfection is not necessary for feeding people. We can start with what seems doable in our context and then listen for the response from volunteers or from the people we serve. There isn't a single right answer to how to create or sustain a food ministry. Each church or community must decide what will work based on what those who are helping are willing to do. People who are food insecure will offer advice on what works and what doesn't. Let's learn to live with the chaos that comes with prioritizing making space for people to volunteer.

DISCUSSION QUESTIONS

1. Which of the four models for including food-insecure volunteers feels most natural for your food ministry, your community, or your congregation? Who in your congregation will help you develop a shared-ministry model? Who will be resistant to the idea?

2. Like Rev. Mary, how willing are you to let go of control or perfection so that others can use their talents to serve? How can you show gratitude to those who serve with you?

3. What first steps can you take so that people who are food insecure can volunteer at your pantry or meal? What can you do to help the food-secure volunteers make space for new volunteers?

SIX

LEADERSHIP TEAMS

When the fight starts at Monday Lunch at The Cathedral Church of St. Paul in Boston, Massachusetts, all eyes turn toward the table by the stairs. The yelling is mostly unintelligible, but we all hear it. Something about a dirty backpack. A tall white man fingers the safety pins that hold the broken zippers of the backpack together. He sways as he yells. A short, unshaven white man at the same table jumps up from his seat, bumps the table, and causes all the drinks to spill. He hollers obscenities, slaps his hand on the table, and begins searching for something in his duffel bag. A third man joins the fray with his fist raised, yelling in Spanish and English.

An African American man across the room starts to stand up; the woman next to him touches his arm, and he sits back down. The MANNA servers pause and then quietly resume delivering the hot plates of food. Jane, wearing jeans, a black shirt, and a name tag identifying her as cathedral staff, appears next to the fighters' table and speaks quietly. A long three minutes pass as the yelling dies down and the three men pick up their belongings and head for the door. The first man turns back to the table, and Rev. Tina Rathbone, wearing a clerical collar, moves to walk with him and says something only he can hear.

They walk together out of the room. Once all three are outside the door, conversation in the room returns to normal.

Fights are rare at food ministries, but they happen. Typically, either other eaters join the fight to support one side or the other or they back away from the action. The people who join the fight often cause bigger problems than the original fighters themselves.

I ask the people at my table whether the men will be kicked out of Monday Lunch.

"Just for this week," a man replies.

"You can't do that here," says a second man.

"But you can always come back," the first man adds.

"I expected other people to join the fight," I said.

"We used to do that," a woman says, "but we learned at the leadership meeting to be pillars of peace."

"Pillars of peace?" I question.

"Yeah. It's our job to keep the peace. If anyone at this table started to go over there, I would have told them no because you don't go joining other people's fights. That's what you do as a pillar of peace."

"You should come to our MANNA leadership meeting" the first man offers. "You could learn about how to do that from Tina."

A LEADERSHIP TEAM

St. Paul's Monday Lunch is run by the MANNA leadership team. Around forty people who are food insecure and five or six food-secure people gather Mondays at 10:00 a.m. to discuss the business of their community and prep for the meal. While the leadership meeting is happening, volunteers from the congregations of alternating suburban churches cook in the kitchen. The Rev. Tina Rathbone, the canon missioner for The Cathedral Church of St. Paul, leads the meeting. On the day that I attend the meeting, the leadership group appears to be made up of mostly white men at first, but additional people trickle in over the next hour, increasing the number of women and people of color.

Tina starts by thanking everyone for coming to this leadership meeting and assures them that "just by being here you have shown leadership." A man in the back mutters as he unpacks and repacks his bag; another man wanders around, going into the bathroom, in and out of the kitchen, down the stairs to the large eating space, and then back to the meeting.

Tina asks the group to review the rules for leadership (one person talks at a time and listening is as important as talking) and the rules for Monday Lunch. One man offers, "Don't drink or use or sell alcohol or drugs." Another says, "No violence or threats of violence." A third man adds, "Even if you are in the right." A man sitting near me leans over to whisper, "That part is hard."

Tina creates the agenda for the meeting using suggestions from the crowd, holding up a finger for each point. "We have to talk about the writers' group and Thanksgiving. Does anyone have anything else?"

Someone hollers, "T-shirts," and she adds it to the agenda.

Tina and the team work out their potluck Thanksgiving Dinner plans by asking specific individuals to take on tasks like table setup and preparing beverages. She asks for people to raise hands if they are bringing a dish and asks a cathedral employee who is present whether they can use the kitchen for reheating.

"Yes, of course," he assures us, and Tina continues with job assignments.

The meeting proceeds through finding a vendor for T-shirts, making plans for the writers' group, and voting on whether to serve hot chocolate inside the doorway to people who are already waiting for today's lunch in the rain. They vote yes. Tina asks for lunch volunteers—people to serve; cleanup; work the coffee, lemonade, and water station; and set up the Eucharist after lunch. After folk have their assignments, she reminds the remainder they will be pillars of peace.

The idea for a leadership team grew out of worship. As part of cathedral staff, Tina attended Monday Lunch in the basement and then celebrated the cathedral's regular 1:00 p.m. Eucharist upstairs in the sanctuary. Each week she provided pastoral care to more than one hundred people at the meal and then left the crowd to provide worship for three to six people. Usually worship included two or three people from the meal and two or three people on their lunch breaks from work at nearby businesses.

Tina said, "Most of the time it was Eddie, Joan, and me, heading upstairs from the meal. Sometimes three others would join us. I was leaving behind the gathered community to have a private Eucharist."

Tina responded first by creating a small worship leadership team. It started with just the three regulars, all food insecure, but grew as she invited other people. After months of working together to plan, set up, and break down the worship service, Tina made a proposal she thought would be most helpful: moving worship downstairs to the same room as the meal. The team, most of whom were eating the meal, voted yes. The meal is now part of worship. "I'm a Eucharist junky," Tina explains, "and that changed the focus of the meal. It was now part of our worship. We moved to where the people were." The leadership team helped clean up the meal in order to make space for the worship that followed.

This changed the lunch ministry. Thinking about Eucharist, which means "thanksgiving," the leadership team decided to create a thank-you dinner for the volunteers from suburban churches who brought the lunch each week. The leadership team raised funds and then cooked the volunteers a fancy dinner with paper tablecloths, invitations, centerpieces, and the menu written out at each seat. In recognition of years and even decades of serving lunch, the leadership team also gave aprons as gifts. The honored volunteers cried in response to the acknowledgment of their work. The leadership team began planning ways to help serve lunch.

CREATING A LEADERSHIP TEAM

A leadership team is a group of people guiding the day-to-day work of a ministry. Typically, a board will handle the finances and supervision of paid staff, while the leadership team works on programming, relationship building, and the details for getting the work done. Board members are selected based on skills in finance and fundraising, including representatives from the congregation. At MANNA and Worcester Fellowship, the leadership teams welcome all and combine learning how to be a leader with the work of leading. In both programs, a few food-secure and many food-insecure volunteers come to the leadership team meeting.

In building a leadership team, it's important to create an environment where people are expected to support others. Tina treats everyone as leaders, starting guidance with phrases like "As leaders we . . ." and by explaining how everyone can be a pillar of peace. She finds that most people will step up to the challenge. Additionally, Tina asks for help in setting up the leadership meetings; she asks people to set up chairs, to make coffee or serve snacks to the team, and to clean up after the meeting. Food can play an important role at a leadership meeting. At Worcester Fellowship, we offer pizza and soda at leadership meetings, and the team grew quickly. Though a full meal isn't necessary, at least offering coffee or water is a sign of hospitality. Generally, when food is available at leadership meetings, more people attend.

Most ministries schedule their leadership team meetings for right before the meal or pantry or right afterward. At Brighton Allston Congregational Church, the meetings are Wednesdays before the meal. But the deacons discuss the pantry on

Sundays—timed purposefully not to coincide with the pantry—because the pantry bylaws require a majority of the decision makers to be church members. Holding a meeting after worship helps with that. At Haywood Street Congregation, a few people are invited to be supporting companions, their equivalent to a leadership team; at MANNA, almost everyone who volunteers is on the team. Alan never came to Worcester Fellowship leadership meetings, but most of the other food-insecure volunteers do. A few of our regular food-secure volunteers come too.

A leadership team can have as much or as little authority as we choose. At the start, the Worcester Fellowship leadership team chose hymns and scripture topics for Bible study. As the team coalesced and took on more responsibilities, they also took on more authority. At MANNA, the initial discussions included procedures for setting the altar for worship. Ultimately, a leadership team should go beyond decision-making and getting the work done. Leadership team meetings can be a place where anyone can bring concerns about the food programs. Persons in attendance can talk through issues and deal with questions about things that occurred in a previous week and events that are coming up. A leadership team meeting is a good place to listen to how people experience the rules and habits of a food ministry. At a Worcester Fellowship discussion about December music, we learned most of the congregation didn't know what Advent is. The leadership meeting provided a place to learn more about one another's religious traditions and about preparing for Christmas.

Leadership meetings should be nonjudgmental spaces where persons can explore and refine the values they want to be expressed in the ministry. Tina talked about "pillars of peace" for years, a little at each meeting, creating a community that all sat quietly when a fight was happening. Interestingly enough, only around forty of more than one hundred persons present for the meal are part of the leadership team, but the whole community had learned the behavior that Tina teaches in the meetings.

The leadership team teaches and models what is discussed in the meetings.

Part of what creates a nonjudgmental space is allowing all topics to be open for discussion. In the early days of Worcester Fellowship, the leadership team took seriously the person who wanted to discuss what toppings we had on the pizza we served at the meetings. This openness to discussing a small topic led the team to taking on more difficult topics over time—such as, what to do with volunteers who always arrive late, how to handle parents who aren't supervising their children, and whether worship should occur before or after lunch. After several years of attending the leadership team meetings at Worcester Fellowship, some women let us know that it was hard for them to access condoms. They didn't want to *ask* for them at church, and food stamps cannot be used to buy them. We accepted their asking as a sign that we had created a nonjudgmental space and put them out on the altar. As the women predicted, no one ever asked for them, but they were always gone by end of worship.

I've had good experiences starting leadership team meetings with scripture, often a text related to an issue we will discuss. I always ask this question after reading the scripture passage: "What did you hear in this text that affects how you lead?" My goal is to get people away from thinking about what they want individually and toward thinking about what is best for the community. As a result, when leadership team members express complaints during the meal or pantry, I ask, "What do you think would be best for everyone?" When leaders are agitated or frustrated, I allow them space to calm down and assure them we will discuss the topic in the leadership meeting.

"Y'all come" meetings—meaning anyone is welcome—result in a regular, core group of attendees along with a wide diversity of people who are new to the meetings or participate intermittently. At Worcester Fellowship we sometimes have people at our meetings who have never been to our lunch or worship. Developing a consistent format for every meeting is helpful for establishing group unity. Everyone at MANNA knows that Tina is going to start the meeting with a review of the definition of a leader and a reminder of the ground rules. After that, they develop an agenda, assign duties, and share a closing prayer.

At Worcester Fellowship, we end each meeting by asking for new business, thus creating the list of topics to discuss at the next meeting—a strategy requested by the regular attendees. This ensures that new attendees can't railroad a new idea through our process. We also identified three value statements that remind us of what we believe: (1) we welcome everyone; (2) we worship outside; and (3) we believe God loves us, as we are, right now. In the beginning I reminded the team of these values when the leaders wanted to restrict the eaters in some way. Eventually, members of the leadership team referred to these values to make their own arguments for keeping a radical welcome.

Worcester Fellowship holds quarterly retreats for its leadership team to learn leadership skills, talk about ongoing issues in the ministry, and practice spiritual disciplines. Members have learned prayer walking, contemplative prayer, and *lectio divina*. One retreat focused on learning one another's names and how best to communicate with team members who are deaf or hearing impaired or for whom English isn't their first language. One year the team studied how to be assertive without being aggressive. Another retreat included practicing being quiet together and listening for the Spirit. Similarly, volunteers at MANNA have done a pilgrimage, walking from Boston to a retreat center in northern Massachusetts, and the CROP walk for hunger and poverty together. They have a weekly Christian meditation group. Nurturing spirituality grows an individual's leadership skills.

In order to build a strong team, assume that the people gathered want to be leaders. From the opening welcome through each discussion, Tina trusts that each person has something to contribute. Sometimes she asks for volunteers; other times she calls on specific people for a certain task. Her confidence in the team is apparent. Worcester Fellowship staff persons assume people volunteering will show up. One Sunday the man who volunteered to read the scripture left before worship, taking the printout of the text, leaving the team scrambling to find a Bible. The fix was to make two printouts, not to stop trusting the team members.

Tina also models calm. As I listened to her listing all the work that needed to get done for Thanksgiving dinner, I found myself in awe of her lack of anxiety. I can imagine myself worrying about whether there would be turkey—but really, is Thanksgiving a failure without it? As the MANNA team planned, there was no drama, no pleading or cajoling, no visible anxiety, but rather a simply stated need and a confident expectation that the people there in the room were capable of meeting that need.

Emily at Haywood Street in Asheville, North Carolina, was similarly unperturbed by problems that developed in the ministry. She knew the people involved and trusted they would find a solution. I visited during a snowstorm, and the volunteers present chatted nervously about whether we would have enough volunteers. Emily simply asked folk what they could do to deal with each issue that came up, and then accepted their answer.

With shared ministry, the leadership is relational. People get to know the team members by name and call on them; they connect with one another on a personal level and not just on the work that needs to be done. At Brighton Allston Congregational Church, the Sunday prayers included prayers for the well-being of leaders who had missed the previous meal, the assumption that it was life's difficulties and not a lack of reliability that caused their absence.

Not all of the shared ministry sites use a leadership team for decision-making. It does provide an opportunity to raise up leaders and to teach our members leadership skills. A leadership team helps send the message that everyone is invited to take on a leadership role, that we haven't simply chosen favorites for the work that needs to be done. The trick to a leadership team is to treat people as leaders and then follow their lead.

DISCUSSION QUESTIONS

1. How can you treat your volunteers as leaders? How can you prepare yourself and your volunteers for the creation of a leadership team? How can you prepare yourself for any opposition you may face?

2. How and when will you gather your volunteers for a leadership meeting? Consider location, food and refreshments, and timing. Who in your food ministry can help you plan or lead the meeting?

3. What types of decisions and discussions need to be brought to your leadership team gatherings? What needs to be changed within your ministry? What rules or by-laws cannot be changed within your ministry? What are your ministry's value statements?

SEVEN

LET VOLUNTEERS LEAD

Dave Holland is in the kitchen of Haywood Street Congregation, singing at the top of his lungs, "Broken halos. . . ." He lifts three huge boxes of potatoes onto the center island of the small kitchen and hands knives to another volunteer and me. "Broken halos that used to shine."[1] He demonstrates cutting a large potato into quarters, cutting a small potato in half, and dropping the pieces in a pan. He then moves to another area to give direction to another set of volunteers as he continues to sing, just one line of the song, over and over again.

Dave is a big white man, balding, with a serious look, and spoon, pan, or a platter always in hand. At 8:00 a.m. at the Downtown Welcome Table in Asheville, North Carolina, volunteers check with Dave for their assignments. Dave is the cook but also the organizer. People ask him about the flowers on the tables, the cloth napkins wrapped around silverware, the special honey butter recipe. Volunteers get the okay to put the hot loaves of bread on the tables, and they look to him when it's time to circle up and pray before the meal. They check with him on food amounts for seconds, when to clear a table for the next seating, whether to wash pans now so they can be reused or leave them until the end of the shift. Dave never stops moving.

Community meals are Sunday and Wednesday, but he spends many more days than that in the new and well-organized commercial kitchen next to the church dining hall.

A volunteer calls through the pass-through between the kitchen and dining room to ask what to do about someone banging on the outside door. "Let him in," Dave replies. As the volunteer heads back to the door, Dave turns to me and says, "I hate for people to wait in the cold." It's 11:00 a.m.; dinner starts at 3:00 p.m.

Dave is beloved to those who know him. His calm manner sets the tone for the crowded bustle of the kitchen. He asks one of the volunteers to make honey butter with the electric mixer, setting up the mixing bowl, measuring the honey by eye, and demonstrating how to slice the five-pound slab of butter. Dave sends an intern to organize the desserts, asks a volunteer in the dining room to fill vases, hands over lemons to be cut up into the water pitchers. When interrupted, he stops, turns to face the speaker, and listens before answering or assigning a new task. As more volunteers come trickling in, Dave calls into the dining room to find out how they are doing or to thank them for coming. Every few minutes he repeats the words to the same song. When I ask about it, he smiles slightly and explains, "It's stuck." Then he turns to check the internal temperature of the baking pork loin.

Dave came to Asheville from Alabama by way of Ohio. He worked for a variety of food service outlets and at a radio station. He says he often felt a call from God to do something different but ignored it. "My life was out of whack. I was miserable and had no direction. I was not doing well, and it wasn't anyone's fault, but one day I was over it." He quit his job and moved into an Asheville hotel. Then, one morning he packed up his belongings and threw them away, heading into the woods nearby. He left the hotel on a Tuesday and ran into Brian Combs, pastor of Haywood Street Congregation, at a shelter on Sunday.

"Did you go to seminary," Dave asked Brian, "or are you just a preacher?"

Brian did go to seminary and so passed Dave's test. After listening to Dave's life story, Brian offered him the opportunity to chop vegetables and move into a bedroom in the church's Respite Ministry. Dave had always wondered if he was called to ministry, and he recognized he'd been given a chance to figure it out. Once at Haywood Street, he helped a few men rebuild the tents they were living in near the railroad tracks and along the river. He cooked. He introduced people he met to Pastor Brian and to Haywood Street Church.

"Life got much better. I was happier. It's been a journey of slowly letting go of a lot of secular life," Dave says.

LEADERS RISE UP

After a year of chopping vegetables, Haywood Street hired Dave as their Banquet Steward. Four years later, he has a private room in the church building, a full-time salary, paid vacation, and benefits. With Dave at the helm, the church added an additional community meal and created a position for an intern reporting to Dave. Pastor Brian's management style has a holistic focus. Paid staff, whether or not they have been homeless, report not only their hours but also what is going on with their health, their exercise, and what they are doing for fun. He asks them about what they are reading and what theological questions they are struggling with. He is on the lookout for how the vicarious trauma caused by the work may lead to compassion fatigue. Dave works forty to sixty hours a week, but if his hours stay high over several weeks, Brian wants to know what he is doing to take a break.

Dave's calling is to create a sense of abundance based on made-from-scratch meals. He never wants the meal to look like it is "seconds" or lower quality food. Each serving bowl or plate is laid out attractively, and the menu is designed to meet a variety of food needs. Dinner for my visit includes a pork loin laid over apples, potatoes roasted with spices, and a celery gravy. There is a vegetarian option, a southern cooked vegetable, small loaves of bread baked on-site, and a kale salad with almonds, cherries, carrots, and cabbage with a cider-vinegar dressing. I ask if folks will eat the kale, and Dave replies, "They are getting used to it. We want to provide healthy food." Along with the healthy food is peach cobbler, which several volunteers tell me is a favorite. At the end of the meal, about half the kale salad is left over; all of the peach cobbler is eaten.

While I'm in the kitchen, volunteers straggle in, most heading to jobs they seem familiar with—setting out napkins, plates, and flatware; making lemonade, coffee, and tea; breaking down boxes; placing flowers, salt, and pepper on each table. Some volunteers are from other churches, some from this congregation, others from the streets. As we get closer to dinner time, Dave calls out, "Butter on aisle seven," and the volunteers pick up the butter dishes, add knives, and place one on each table. Dave drives the entire meal, but he is also the bottleneck. Anyone who is new has to wait for direction from Dave, and the regulars ask him about every variation from the norm.

"Fourteen cups of flour" repeats Dave, four times, for each batch of bread the intern is making. There isn't a written recipe. Additionally, he figures out how to unclog the sink, finds more drinking glasses, remembers where the lemons are stored, and more. Both volunteers and staff run everything by Dave. This slows everyone down but creates time for conversation. Volunteers call one another by name, check in about doctors' appointments and worn-out cars, their kids, and how their week is going.

FINDING YOUR LEADERS

All communities have leaders. Finding leaders starts by noticing who other people are following. If people are following someone, then that person has the skills and knowledge to draw others. Ultimately, the people who are food insecure can tell who the leaders are. Dave at Haywood Street is a natural leader, as was Alan at Worcester Fellowship. Most of the shared-ministry sites I visited had at least one natural leader in an important role in their ministry. It is not clear whether the churches found the leaders or the leaders found the churches, but because ministries were open to including eaters in their program, important leaders found their place.

When looking for leaders, we must remember that our internal biases may cause us to look for leadership qualities in certain people while missing those same qualities in others. Our North American society tends to assume that leaders are men more than women, whites more than people of color, people without visible disabilities more than people who appear differently abled, and middle-class people more than people who are poor. Large numbers of people—mostly those who don't look like our society's stereotype of a "leader"—have been told their weaknesses are more important than their strengths.

People who do not have adequate access to food are often treated by our society and by meals programs and pantries as if they do not know about food distribution. We presume people eating at meals and shopping at pantries don't have the skills necessary to acquire food rather than understanding the systemic barriers preventing equal access. Or we just don't think about it. This keeps us from recognizing the skills people do have. Some of what we must do to counteract that attitude is to be willing to give up the power of running food ministries the way we want to. We have to remember that we don't have a better grasp on what needs to happen just because we have enough food. Personally, I see myself as a great organizer, but that doesn't mean I'm the *only* organizer. And that doesn't mean I know more about organizing food than the people who come to eat. When I make space for others to share their gifts, talents, and wisdom, the ministry improves.

Leadership is not a limited commodity. As we saw with leadership teams, people's gifts grow as we give them the opportunity to lead. When we develop partnerships, leadership thrives. When the goal is maximum participation, many people demonstrate their gifts and leadership. Imagine if we evaluated direct-service ministries based on the number of people encouraged to use their gifts rather than efficiency, order, or pounds of food distributed.

As long as the rules require that only some people can serve and only some people can eat, the community will be divided. Recognizing gifts and skills and inviting people to volunteer leads to an increased sense of belonging. As we learned in chapter five, the act of volunteering moves us from being a guest to being part of the community. Without the rights of leadership, the people who come to receive food do not have full rights of membership in the community. Shared ministry intentionally expands the rights of leadership to people with and without food security.

At St. James, the woman who directs the pantry needs the food the pantry distributes, and she works alongside the pastor to keep the pantry running. Her gifts include being detail oriented, organized, and orderly. The pastor, on the other hand, is welcoming, flexible, and spontaneous. A volunteer commented that the pantry director sets the rules for the pantry, and the pastor builds the relationships. The volunteers appreciate that there is one person they can go to for enforcement of rules and another they can go to for flexibility. At all of the ministries I visited, the leaders who rose up had skills that complement those of the pastors.

At Hope Lutheran Church in Reading, Pennsylvania, the food pantry has two lead volunteers: one who is more organized and does the ordering and another who is more charismatic and guides the distribution while the pantry is open. They both step in whenever a problem arises. One is bilingual and can speak with the non-English-speaking shoppers while the other resolves problems between volunteers and the shoppers. This means the pastor can work elsewhere while the pantry is open, although she checks in periodically to visit with the shoppers. Hope's Table has a cook but not a director, which requires the pastor to be more engaged in serving the food.

Brighton Allston Congregational has a volunteer cook, a food pantry coordinator, and a meal coordinator, all people who are or have been food insecure, although the pastor plays an organizing role as well. MANNA in Boston pays a stipend to two people to coordinate their Monday meal. The Cathedral Church of St. Paul also hired three previously homeless men as full-time sextons. The lack of a volunteer in the director role for Chat and Chew in Philadelphia leaves the organizational work to the rector.

These leaders were "found" rather than "developed." Each church that I visited with a significant leader first started a ministry without a leader, invited participants to volunteer, and as the ministry developed, a leader—or several—appeared. The leadership role was then sculpted to fit the person doing the leading. So at some ministries a leader may cook and organize; at another, the leader may only cook or may play a different role. If there is a similarity between these leaders, it is that the people who have been food insecure tend to be stricter with the rules than those who have not, although even that is not universal. The art of the ministry is in recognizing when someone has the skills to take a leadership role and then defining the position in such a way that he or she succeeds. This results in a different kind of leader in each location.

While I didn't see any church train someone to be a leader, most churches were intentional in creating an environment where a leader could rise up. The people who started the food ministries spent time getting to know people and then invited them to do the work. They noticed the skills of the volunteers, looking for persons who stood out and who other volunteers seemed to look to for help or guidance. These volunteers had earned the respect of their peers and were already on their way to becoming leaders.

But in looking for leaders, we must be careful not to ask persons to overextend themselves. Life in poverty is exhausting, and we should remind people to take breaks when needed. One of the rules at Worcester Fellowship is that it's always OK to say no. We want to build people up and set them up for success. Asking someone to take on a job that is too big or too difficult can lead to a sense of defeat if he or she fails. Start by giving people small tasks and notice if they succeed. Honor successes in ways that respect people's wishes—some love to be recognized in front of everyone while others like to remain behind the scenes. Once we identify a person or two as organizers, coordinators, or cooks, we can show them respect by allowing them to make real decisions and trusting them to do their best. We can find a balance between the goals of our programs and our flexibility for change. We can let people set their own goals while also having a backup plan so mistakes do not devastate our leaders or injure our programs.

Most of the programs I visited did not require long-term sobriety or resolution of mental health challenges in order to volunteer, but the programs did look for certain traits or behaviors in persons performing certain tasks. For example, people working in food prep must have clean hands, be able to stand for long periods of time, and not be sneezing or coughing. People welcoming at the entrance must be friendly and in control of the language they use. Steady hands are necessary for serving coffee or other drinks. Worship leaders need to be able to speak clearly. In some programs, paid positions might require sobriety or at least a level of reliability. Cleanup, on the other hand, can be done by anyone who has come to work that day. Most importantly, set the same requirements for those who are food secure and those who are not.

We can expand who we permit to be leaders in our ministries simply by noticing the people who lead others. Invite people in; ask for help. The hardest part may be in letting go of how we think a task should be done. Once we believe that there are leaders all around us, waiting to be found, they will appear. Like Dave, some will serve as the leaders of whole programs, while others will simply be sure the floor is cleaned when there is a spill. All who volunteer will be encouraged by the way we notice the work that they do.

DISCUSSION QUESTIONS

1. What stereotypes or internal biases do you have about the characteristics of a successful leader? How or where did you learn those stereotypes? How do your biases affect how you choose leaders for your ministry?

2. What skills are needed to be a leader in your particular ministry?

3. What kind of support can you provide to a person who has stepped up to lead a part of your meal or pantry?

EIGHT

LIVING WITH CHAOS

S hared ministry works, but it isn't always efficient. It is not organized. The most honest description of shared ministry is chaotic. Creating a shared-ministry environment is full of obstacles. Well run, long-standing, effective shared ministries continue to face challenges. Despite the opportunities to get to know one another, many volunteers work alone. Most but not all of the volunteers are skilled; it is difficult to supervise the large numbers, so those without adequate skills are often not redirected. Some of the inefficiencies lead to waste. Shared ministry may add chaos to the everyday logistical challenges of getting food ready and delivered to large groups of people with many different needs.

In my doctor of ministry project, I set out to show how shared ministry could cross the barriers between people who are food secure and insecure. I assumed people would work with, interact with, and build solidarity with people who are very different from themselves. I believed that the relationships built in shared ministry would lead to motivation to engage in community redevelopment and systems change. I suggested that shared ministry could lead individuals to rise to the challenge of overcoming systemic racism, classism, sexism, and ableism.

I was naive.

However, shared ministry did build relationships, and it did cross boundaries of race, class, gender, and ability. And chaos is not disaster. People were fed and were able to pick up groceries they needed. The chaos makes space for creativity and change. Shared ministry allows everyone to be involved in problem-solving. When I start to feel overwhelmed by the chaos created by shared ministry, I remind myself that God created our world out of chaos.

CHALLENGES IN SHARED MINISTRY

While volunteering at a food ministry requires people to inter-act with others of different races, classes, and abilities and to develop connections with people they might not meet otherwise, these interactions can be rough. In private interviews, volunteers expressed concerns that their racial or ethnic heritage was not appreciated or that people of another race were shown privilege over others. A few people openly criticized people with mental and physical limitations. People who were food secure gained some appreciation for the challenges of poverty, but that did not lead them to push for systemic change. The work is imperfect.

In some cases, these issues arose because volunteers often worked alone and were not building relationships with their fellow volunteers. One person supervised a distribution table; one person chopped a vegetable; one person made dessert. Though the work of keeping a food ministry open and operational was shared, many tasks were done alone. Working together separately keeps relationships to a minimum and prevents connections beyond a superficial level. Meals and worship mitigated some of that separateness, but for the actual tasks, many volunteers did not interact with others. I could see connections being made, jokes shared, a person checking in on someone else, but the attitudes were tentative, cautious, and careful.

Many volunteers did not know the names of the other volunteers. I had imagined people building solidarity and changing the world together; in reality, most volunteers moved from being unknown to one another to being acquaintances.

While the majority of the volunteers were assigned—or chose—tasks they did well, some were not effective or skilled. Because people work alone, most of the poor work went unnoticed. This rarely hurt the goal of handing out food but sometimes led to other volunteers complaining. One man assigned to the job of "hospitality" had a monotone voice that made him seem angry as he handed out cookies. Several people at distribution tables ignored shoppers rather than helping them or stopping them from taking extra. A few volunteers gave extras to their friends. Some didn't see when a shopper took more than the allotted portion. People assigned to oversight responsibilities, such as determining serving sizes or the order for food distribution, got lost in the details and couldn't make good decisions. One pantry volunteer disrupted the line of shoppers in the effort to speed up the process. Another young man insisted people must take food that they'd said they didn't want. Pantries have various systems to identify how much food each person can pick up, but volunteers did not always ask for the tokens that identified household size. Whether volunteers were moving into a corner for a nap, spending time wandering instead of at their station, or out for a cigarette when the program was at it busiest, there were people who were not working when they were supposed to be.

The overall approach everywhere I visited was to let people be. The ministries weren't necessarily offering training, though new volunteers, including me, were shown once how to do the assigned task. Sometimes a volunteer would complain about another volunteer's work, and that volunteer would be reassigned. (Shoppers and eaters rarely comment.) A few places created an extra role—someone to notice unfilled gaps—but few places confronted nonperformers. Some volunteers wandered away from tasks they couldn't do, and only a few asked for different assignments.

EFFICIENCY

The more volunteers, the more people we have invited into community. But at some point, more volunteers result in more chaos. Shared ministry prioritizes having work for everyone who wants it over working efficiently. I visited two meals at Trinity Memorial Church in Philadelphia, Sanctuary Angels, a meal run by food-secure volunteers feeding people who are food insecure, and Chat and Chew, a shared-ministry program. The difference between the quiet, reflective Sanctuary Angels meal and the noise and energy at the shared ministry of Chat and Chew could not have been more dramatic. Sanctuary Angels employs one or two cooks who also clean, an artist for the programming, and the pastor. They provide exactly enough food; the meal, meditation, and art program start promptly; and the workers leave the building on schedule. By contrast, Chat and Chew is slow to get started and takes five to seven people to cook, four to six to set the table, and all twelve to clean up. It rarely ends on time.

Traditional direct-service meal programs are much more efficient than shared-ministry programs. Two cooks and four or five volunteers can setup, serve a crowd (even a large one), enforce the meal's rules, and clean up. That efficiency ensures that people get their first serving before others get their third, that latecomers can find a seat, and that every drop of spaghetti is served. In comparison, shared ministry is chaotic and inefficient.

At shared-ministry food pantries, items that should have been bagged were served loose, while other items were left in their boxes rather than given out individually. Shoppers sometimes had to show their number or their family size repeatedly or not at all. Restrictions on how many items a household could take sometimes resulted in items left over at the end. Food was handed out that was unlabeled. At one pantry, I handed out bags of white gravy for an hour and then was told it was creamy Italian salad dressing. Workers would spend time carrying food into basements or storage sites only for the next crew to bring it back out a few hours later. Boxes of canned food were opened and the cans laid out for display only to be moved to a different table.

At shared-ministry meals, the largest inefficiency was duplication of effort. Though inefficient to have multiple people set tables or serve the same food item, this "inefficiency" allows more people to volunteer. One person might cut the dessert portions, the next place them on plates, and a third decide the pieces are too big and cut each one in half again. The volunteer cook's last-minute decision to have croutons meant two people watching a two-slice toaster and then cutting bread slices into squares.

Some of the problems of shared ministry are the same as the problems in any food pantry or meal program. One meal program struggled with bedbugs coming into their space through backpacks and sweaters. They treated the edge of the room and required people to leave backpacks there, but people were nervous their things would be stolen. Every meal program encounters a day when the dishwasher doesn't work or the oven isn't turned on when the casserole is put in. Every pantry has a day with twenty extra turkeys or a day when there aren't enough. It is common for someone to lose something or to have something stolen. One church doesn't have recycling pickup for the large number of empty boxes produced by their food pantry. There were meals with no vegetarian option or with mostly carbohydrates. Every meal program has its occasional fight and regular complaining about what is offered or not available. People are accidentally passed over; someone takes extra.

The trick to shared ministry is to accept that chaos is inevitable and that the goal is creating relationships. Requiring expertise in volunteers can limit who can be part of the ministry.

There are certainly areas where skill is critical—a cook must know how to prepare meals, anyone who handles food must follow ServSafe regulations—but many tasks don't have to be done perfectly. As the saying goes, done is better than perfect. While there are instances where offering training can be helpful and positive, the open nature of shared ministry means that people who have been constantly criticized and redirected and told they don't know enough are welcome in these programs. It's worth it to have some people take an extra can of peas because you let someone who can't look people in the eye have a turn volunteering at the canned food station.

FACING PRESSURE

All those who work in ministry face pressure to make their outreach efficient and expandable. This pressure may come from websites evaluating charities, from members of the church sponsoring the ministry, from funders giving their money, and even from participants in the program itself. But shared ministry doesn't prioritize efficiency. When efficiency is more important than relationships and the individuals we meet, we end up with programs imposing change on the people we serve. Focusing on relationships enables volunteers to own the program and allows eaters and shoppers to contribute their values and knowledge. The fact is, if we prioritize relationships, efficiency is unlikely to follow. More relational ministries require more volunteers and more time while perhaps delivering less food. Relationships are not efficient; relationships are messy and constantly changing. For shared ministry to improve upon direct-service ministry, the focus must be on relationship building rather than on efficiency. Inefficiency and chaos create opportunities for volunteering. Shared ministry encourages finding a role for every person who wants to volunteer and asking every person to contribute to feeding their neighbors.

To meet the needs of donors and to qualify for grant funding, ministries may become focused on efficiency and order to prioritize limiting waste. When that is the focus, people with expendable money and time may feel good about themselves, but this focus does not make space for people who are food insecure to volunteer, much less to be engaged in the decision-making. Most grants ask for evidence that a ministry is feeding the most people or providing the most pounds of food for the least amount of money. Funders want quick, efficient solutions and stories of measurable change in people's lives. But those ministries that have focused on building relationships may find it difficult to treat one of their volunteers or eaters as marketing material for a grant application or for fundraising.

DEALING WITH FOOD WASTE

During my visits to food ministries, I almost always observed some amount of waste. At more than one food pantry, cases of frozen food were accidentally defrosted and then thrown away. Food received from food banks and area businesses usually is left over from what could be sold. The food needs to be sorted to separate the rotten from the fresh. I saw cakes with mold, burst fruit, and overly soft vegetables. Stores donate massive amounts of pastries and breads, some past their prime, meaning volunteers spent a fair amount of time sorting out the expired pieces. If a volunteer person found, for example, a rock-hard baguette, the whole case might be thrown out, even though the rest was still good.

As a person who hates waste, seeing what was thrown away was upsetting. It wasn't until long after my visits, as I was learning more about food banks, that I realized that food banks are efficient at converting grocery store and food production waste into resources for people who are hungry. One of their goals is to provide a way for people with food waste to give it away. All the defrosted frozen vegetables I saw thrown away were destined for the dump before the food bank accepted them as a donation. At one pantry, the oranges donated were so old that we threw away a third before bagging and distribution. They were waste before we received them. Shared ministry didn't increase the waste.

Still, I grimaced at spilled pitchers of coffee and lemonade, filled cups that were never drunk, milk that sat out on tables, sugar and creamer on the floors. There are always a few people who take huge servings and then throw most of it away. Serving people at their seats is gracious, but people get too much of a food they won't eat. When served family style, people taking what they want from a serving bowl, there is still too much food at each table. Buffet lines reduce waste but reduce opportunities for relationship building as well.

Likewise, at my earliest visits to food pantries, I was anxious about volunteers giving some people extras or not noticing when shoppers took more than the allowed amounts. Pastors often knew when people were recovering from an illness or having a hard time and gave them something extra. Some volunteers were stricter with people they suspected of cheating the system. But no matter who was distributing or what system they were using, the food was never evenly shared.

Over time it became obvious to me that no distribution system can be completely "fair." First, not everyone wants every item, and often there is not enough of an item for each person to have one. It was common for the food bank to provide just a few of several types of an item: for example, in a hundred bags of bread, ten would be whole wheat, twenty hamburger buns, six packages of English muffins, and so on. With ninety shoppers, the early people got more choices, but those shopping later got more than one bag of bread. Inevitably, someone wanting English muffins but receiving only a baguette will feel shortchanged.

Second, there is no way for the pantry managers to know exactly how many people will be coming each week, much less which foods the shoppers will want more of. Even pantries where the staff hands people the food items (rather than allowing users to shop for themselves), the quantities they offer need to be changed as they see how the day develops. The goal is to practice equality but also to reduce the amount of leftover food. The two ideas are incompatible. Therefore, pantries hand out smaller and smaller portions of popular items as the day goes on and larger and larger portions of less desired items. The Food for All pantry at St. James improves the fairness of this by allowing the last people, who get the least choice, to also be the people who can go back through the pantry to pick through the leftovers. I wanted to emphasize fairness over avoiding leftovers, but of course that would make me uncomfortable because the leftovers would be waste.

RULES OR NO RULES

My discomfort caused by some of the practices of the food ministries I visited does not mean that those ministries should change what they are doing. The goal is not to reaffirm my values nor to teach thrift, self-discipline, ambition, or other similar values. We do not want to prioritize waiting in line or soft-spokenness as more important than creativity or joy. The goal is to provide food and to grow relationships. When we develop rules for our ministries, we need to evaluate what they accomplish. Rules that make sure everyone gets closer to a fair share are valuable; those that simply reinforce a particular set of values are not. Ministries that receive food from food banks may need to set rules for shoppers to qualify; ministries that do not receive food from food banks or who turn down federal foods may choose to be open to anyone without financial tests. I visited a traditional meal program where a person couldn't eat if he or she wore a hat or had an umbrella on the table. We should ask ourselves what our rules are accomplishing and who we aren't welcoming based on them.

Shared ministry avoids requiring a pre-determined set of behaviors to take part. There are no rules about what clothing is acceptable or how people should talk or act, beyond rules that create safety for others. The shared-ministry programs I visited expand the leadership table by following the voices of those on the margins. Even knowing that and wanting that does not necessarily overcome the way my heart wants people to follow my own set of values. I like people to follow rules, to wait patiently, to address me politely, to say thank you and please. My learning has been to relax, to listen for people's intent and meaning, to not take offense quite so easily.

I've tried not only to resist the temptation to solve everything with rules but also to resist the temptation to have no rules, thereby creating a free-for-all. In the first few years of Worcester Fellowship, I loved what I called "the theology of the sandwich"—that is, the way our Communion service ended so that the bread and juice on the altar were transformed into peanut butter and jelly sandwiches. Like the bread and juice, I wanted everyone to come forward around the table and take what they needed. When we had six to eight people at worship and twenty sandwiches, that worked wonderfully. When we grew to ten people and then to twenty, it still worked well. We said, "Take what you need." One person took one sandwich, and another person split his sandwich with someone else. One or two people took three or five sandwiches.

When Worcester Fellowship grew to thirty and then to fifty and then to a hundred people at lunch, the leaders of the congregation demanded order. The fact that we never ran out of lunches was irrelevant. Volunteers and eaters noticed some people had three sandwiches and others only had one. It felt unfair. First the leadership team asked, then begged, for a lunch line. Eventually I listened to the pleas of the leaders and accepted the idea that perhaps I didn't know what was best. We instituted a line. Eventually I learned to listen to other things as well. We stopped having only peanut butter and jelly. People wanted bologna and ham and tuna. They were not interested in my argument that bologna ruined my Eucharist analogy, and I set it aside in favor of the leadership team's knowledge of what the community really needed.

EFFECTIVE NOT EFFICIENT

Ultimately, we hope our meals programs can be effective—if not efficient. How do we do this? By creating reasonable rules and then holding them lightly. Perhaps think of rules as guidelines. At places with both a pastor and a director, the director was able to be more rules oriented, while attending to logistics of the setup, serving or shopping, and cleanup. It matters, for example, that there are the right number of tables and that the event starts on time. The pastor was then freed up to connect to people, building relationships, making exceptions to the rules for people who had special circumstances. Volunteers, eaters, and shoppers appreciated both roles. It is more difficult if the pastor is also trying to coordinate organizational activities. It is important that all the leaders hold the rules lightly.

We can pass on as much authority as we can to the volunteers. While our rules may limit how much of an item each shopper can take, allowing the volunteer at the distribution table the authority to make or break that rule helps to build the leadership skills of the volunteers. At the places I visited, volunteers had the authority to ask participants to wait for their turn, to stop shouting, to put something back, to de-escalate a fight, or to refer someone to the leadership to get special treatment. Volunteers can decide how the table should be set, which beverages are offered, whether one person needs a few extra carrots. Sharing the authority honors the work the volunteers do.

While there are many challenges to sharing the work at a direct-service food ministry, the benefits outweigh the problems. People want to volunteer; many have some or all skills needed to be volunteers. In Matthew 25:31-46, the nations are judged as either sheep or goats based on their choice to provide food and other material resources to people who need them. In Acts 6:1-7 when the widows are overlooked and perhaps do not get a turn to serve, this creates conflict in the community. Shared ministry helps us meet the biblical mandate of feeding people and allowing everyone the chance to serve. This is chaotic, inefficient, and invaluable.

DISCUSSION QUESTIONS

1. Do you struggle with chaos? If so, why? Do you appreciate chaos? If so, why? How would you explain the value of chaos to people who assume that chaos equals a lack of effectiveness?

2. What is the importance of efficiency in your ministry? How do you balance feeding people efficiently with the chaos of building relationships?

3. What are the top three values of your food pantry or meal program? How do they affect the rules that you put in place and how you choose to enforce them?

NINE

UNEXPECTED LEARNINGS

Each Sunday, I arrived at Worcester Fellowship with the knowledge and trust that Alan would have lunch under control. On the rare weeks he didn't show up, the other volunteers had learned his style and would step in and make things work well enough. The weeks he was there, the Worcester Fellowship staff spent time on pastoral care, worship leadership, and meeting new people in the lunch line. Alan allowed us to think about ministry instead of lunch.

In fact, I wasn't thinking about lunch at all that Sunday when it happened. I arrived on time, maybe a bit early. I'd preached that morning at an indoor church, telling the congregation about Worcester Fellowship. I'd been off the previous week, so I didn't know the good news: Alan had been hired as a floor clerk at Home Depot. If I'd known, I'd have been worried about who would be our next lunch leader. But I'd missed the good news, and I was thinking about my Worcester Fellowship sermon.

Georgeanne, another co-pastor at Worcester Fellowship, met me at my car. This was unusual because we'd developed a system of not helping each other. The more we left for people who attended church to do, the more they felt involved. Usually when I arrived, I would walk across the street to ask who could help me unload the lunches from my car. Volunteers would help me unload the hot cocoa and water coolers, a couple of folding tables, and any donations of socks, hats, or gloves that had accumulated in my trunk.

But this week Georgeanne was right there as I stepped out of the car.

"Alan is dead." Georgeanne announced. "I'm sorry to be so blunt, but I heard that Alan is dead."

"Alan who?" I asked slowly. I couldn't wrap my mind around what she was saying.

"Alan who runs lunch."

"What happened?"

"He was celebrating his job at the bus station."

"He got a job at the bus station?" I didn't mean to be obstinate.

"You weren't here last week. Alan got a job at Home Depot. He was supposed to start tomorrow. I guess a bunch of guys got together last night to celebrate. They were at the bus station, and they were drinking and who knows what else. Tom says that Alan fell down the stairs and died."

"He's sure that it was our Alan?" I'd heard deaths reported before and even gone to identify the body of our parishioners. But sometimes our sources would be wrong, and our parishioner would be alive. I didn't want this news to be true.

"Tom knows Alan, Liz. He's dead."

I couldn't even cry. I was numb. "What are we going to do about lunch?"

"Tom is unloading the lunches the church has brought, but I don't know what we are going to do." As Georgeanne and I continued talking, a group of Worcester Fellowship regulars gathered around my car.

"I guess we should get unloaded," I said.

One of the volunteers added, "Alan would tell us to get to work."

So we unloaded, set up, served lunch, and worshiped together. At Bible study, we invited people to share memories of Alan. The next week, we held a memorial service.

DEFINING SUCCESS

As a leader of Worcester Fellowship, I spent a lot of time lowering the expectations of the food-secure volunteers about the outcomes that could be accomplished through our work. When people asked for our success stories, I knew they hoped for stories that went like this: Someone hears about Worcester Fellowship, begins worshiping with us, gets sober, and finds housing. People also hope to hear that someone got away from an abuser or obtained mental health services. The people who support Worcester Fellowship would be happy with stories that seem small: someone qualifying for disability, getting into a recovery program, or just admitting the need for mental health treatment.

But most of our success stories are even smaller than that. A man attends Worcester Fellowship for years, but only when he is sober. One Sunday, he comes while drunk and realizes he is still welcome. A woman tells us she is abused. She doesn't leave her abuser or get help, but she feels relief and acceptance in telling us. A man who has been trying to get permission to see his child more often is told that he can have limited to supervised visits, and he asks me to be the supervisor.

During worship at Worcester Fellowship, we celebrate people who have found work. These celebrations are part of our praise reports—a time for reporting how we have seen God at work in our lives—and we make a big deal about them. We honor milestones in recovery of all kinds—from addictions, from violence—and we give out tokens for one day; for one week; for one month; for two, three, four, five, six, seven, eight, nine, ten weeks; or for months or years. We celebrate each of these markers, knowing that people often go back to the drinking, to the drugs, to the violence they inflict, and to the violence they receive.

We also hold many memorial services. Drinking kills. Drugs kill. People—some sober and clean and some who are using—are killed by other people using alcohol or drugs. People die of the cold and of the heat. People get cancer and diabetes and pneumonia. When the people who die are volunteers in our ministry, it feels like a more significant failure. These volunteers have used their skills to make a better place for other people. They volunteered because they cared about the needs of others. Alan never admitted to being homeless, but others told us he slept at the bus station. Even so, he talked about people who didn't have homes as "those people." He loved "those people" and wanted to help them, but he didn't see himself as one of them. He saw himself as the helper, not the helpee.

It hurts worse to do a memorial service for our volunteers because we know them in a way we don't know many of the attendees. We know the gifts that are lost to the world, and we know their dreams of who they might have become. We know the things they were working on, the things they hoped to do next week and next month. Everyone who dies is a child of God, but we know the volunteers as siblings in Christ.

As I noted in chapter seven, food ministries don't so much create leaders as notice them and give them the authority to do what they already know how to do. Worcester Fellowship did not discover another lunch manager to replace Alan for several years. People stepped up to one or another of Alan's jobs—putting lunches aside for latecomers or handing lunches to folk who weren't willing to come near our gathering. Some tried to tell other volunteers how to do their work, but even if they were saying the same things that Alan said, they weren't respected and trusted the way Alan was. We kept the changes that Alan had made to our lunch line, but we didn't continue with the constant tinkering to make things better. Having a leader like Alan wasn't a necessity for Worcester Fellowship, but his wisdom and willingness to work were invaluable. Without a leader like Alan, the pastors and pastoral care volunteers spent much of lunchtime organizing the meal rather than visiting. When pastoral care leaders are handing out lunches, it takes longer to move from transactional to relational connections.

SHARED MINISTRY IS JUST THE BEGINNING

Although not nearly as painful as Alan's death, my doctor of ministry research results were also a disappointment. I'd set out to show that by engaging in shared ministry, volunteers would engage with people of differing levels of food security and would help overcome the boundaries created by oppression. I hypothesized that "shared ministry attends to power dynamics: to oppression and domination."[1] I imagined volunteers would work together, get to know one another, and build deep connections that would lead to deep conversations about the causes of poverty and to the actions that would change them. I wrote about Gutiérrez's theory that as we learn about oppression, we eventually feel solidarity with people who are poor. I believed in the idea that in knowing one another, volunteers would become advocates for changing systems. And then I set out to visit churches who employed shared ministry in their food programs.

The visits were delightful. I found volunteers who deeply valued the chance to help with the food ministries and who were excited to tell me how well their program worked. I found leaders who were excited by the practice of shared ministry and who were including food-insecure people in every part of their programming. I met with leaders of the county food bank as they asked Paula from Food for All for advice on how to get other pantries and meals to include people who are food insecure as volunteers.

I was excited that all these churches had done exactly what Gustavo Gutiérrez and other scholars said they should do: They started with the people who needed material resources, and they got to know them. Their primary question was not "What can we do?" but "What are the skills of this community?" The lead organizers and staff knew the people they were serving—not only their names but also what was going on in their families, how were they were getting by, and what they hoped and dreamed and feared.

What I didn't see was food-secure people and food-insecure people working together to change the systems that cause poverty. Many volunteers couldn't remember one another's names. People were more connected across race and class but were still wary of one another. People who had been volunteering for months or years would point to another volunteer and say, "She comes all the time. Make sure she doesn't steal anything." My idea that working together would lead people to being in solidarity and overcoming racism and classism was idealistic. Volunteer interviews included many people who could not name more than one other person in the program.

My results surprised and disappointed me. Upon reflection, they shouldn't have. In indoor churches where I've served, many people didn't know one another. Most people in churches share little more than comments about the weather during coffee hour. There may be small groups of close friends in churches, but most of these groups do not cross racial or class boundaries. In the food ministries, people may care about others' well-being, but that does not mean they are close friends or that they know details about one another's lives. Similarly, when I volunteer for mission projects, I learn the skills of the people I work with without always knowing their names or much about their lives. I was looking for food ministry to be different from the world around it. For the most part, neither food ministry nor church manages to perfect the world.

That is not to say that superficial relationships between volunteers at food ministries don't make a difference in the lives of individuals. I saw more cross-racial and cross-class dialogue and engagement within the food ministries than in most traditional churches I have visited. Volunteers at the food programs universally felt appreciated for their work and felt like others recognized their gifts. They even felt welcome to be part of the sponsoring church and described a sense of belonging. They felt pride in the work they were doing and in caring for others.

Similarly, it was clear Alan belonged in Worcester Fellowship. He hung out with us for more than the chance to manage lunch; he came earlier than he needed to and stayed later than was necessary. He made small talk with the leadership members, the volunteers, and with those who had come to eat. He was quick with a joke, and he appreciated getting an opportunity to be in charge. Shared ministry doesn't overcome the biases society imposes around race or class or create a perfect community, but it can change one community. And that makes the world a better place.

When Alan died, so did my belief that allowing food-insecure persons—or persons who are homeless or persons with addictions—to volunteer would be the solution to poverty. Yes, volunteering allows people to feel recognized for their skills. Volunteers at Worcester Fellowship discovered skills inside themselves that they didn't know they had, and they used those skills to find paid work. Alan even used his time volunteering as a way to explain the gaps in his work record. But volunteering is not sufficient for ending poverty. Or homelessness. Or addiction. It certainly does not end oppression, even on a small scale. My doctor of ministry project suggested shared ministry would change the world (and perhaps every doctoral student dreams of that), but it does not. Yet shared ministry did do something that I didn't expect: It created church. Volunteering is belonging. People became interconnected with one another when they worked together. And being interconnected while eating together in God's house creates church.

DISCUSSION QUESTIONS

1. What unrealistic goals have you set for your food ministry or for your church? What did you do when you realized the goals were unattainable?

2. How do you evaluate the success of your ministry?

3. When tragedy strikes your ministry, how can you care for yourself and for your fellow partners in ministry?

PART THREE

CREATE CHURCH

TEN

INTERDEPENDENCE

The worst thing is the offering plate when you can't put some-thing in," Selena tells me as she washes dishes in the church kitchen. "But I can help with the cooking and cleaning, so I have found my place." The women at Chat and Chew at Trinity Memo-rial in Philadelphia, Pennsylvania, have just finished their St. Patrick's Day dinner. Twelve residents of a nearby women's shel-ter, two pastors, another volunteer, and I made corned beef and cabbage, pistachio pudding, and "Irish potatoes," a local des-sert. We cooked, ate, and then cleaned up together. "It's a fun chance to do some cooking, which in our situation is not very often possible," Selena explains to me.

This shared cooking experience is a joint ministry of Trin-ity Memorial Church and the Welcome Church. When I arrived, the tiny kitchen counter was overflowing with bags of vegeta-bles, pudding mix, and beverages. Trinity's rector, Rev. Donna L. Maree, was already boiling water for potatoes. She pointed to foods that needed prep and asked for volunteers to take on various tasks. The women were eager to help but not quick to notice what needed to be done. Schaunel Steinnagel, a pastor from the Welcome Church, cut up fruit and visited with Sandra, who made the pudding.

A few women declared with authority that they knew the correct way to make tea or to cut the bread. Donna assigned the less assertive women jobs of cutting fruit, finding serving bowls, and chopping potatoes. While I cut up pineapple for the fruit salad, I met Selena, who asked me about my research and eagerly took on teaching me about Chat and Chew. "The menu has to be what can be made, consumed, and cleaned up in two hours." As I moved on to cantaloupe, Selena continued, "I love volunteering. I've been volunteering since I was in high school. I'm willing to give my time to any cause. I give my time instead of money that I don't have."

The tiny space created intimacy; everyone shifted places when someone needed to use the sink, find a knife, or get a cutting board. Requests, such as "Can you put this in the sink?" and "Hand me the rest of the potatoes," were intermixed with friendly questions, such as "How was your day?" and "What are you doing this weekend?"

Down the hall through Donna's office and into the church parlor, four more women organized the serving buffet. They put out chairs along two tables, leaving space between each chair for rolling bags, suitcases, and backpacks. One woman put the silverware drawer on her walker and worked her way slowly around the table, setting a knife, fork, and spoon at each place. One woman moved between the kitchen and parlor, making iced tea, coffee, and hot tea.

When dinner was ready, we stood for grace and then served ourselves from the buffet. Donna sat in the middle and kept up conversation with the people around her, sometimes telling stories, other times asking folk about their days. Some women did not talk. Two women were interested in the fact that I was from the Boston area and shared stories of people they knew there. As we got up to serve ourselves seconds and dessert, Donna and Schaunel guided the women in planning the April menu.

As we got up to clear the tables and clean up the space, Selena commanded others to clear their own place setting as she stacked the dishes on a rolling cart. As Selena and I walked together toward the kitchen, she said to me, "In the end, all the work gets done. But I know some people aren't going to do anything." She started to unload the dishes into the sink and then added, "No one really pulls in the folk who fade into the background, and that's aggravating."

Donna was busy the whole time, pointing out where the linens were stored, deciding what needed to be washed, finding dish soap, and identifying where to put things away. As cleanup wound down, women arranged rides, hurried out to catch a bus, or lingered, finding additional helpful tasks or starting new conversations. They hung out as much to be together as to help.

MAKING SPACE

Trinity Memorial Church is a large building at the corner of a pleasant neighborhood, just outside the historic district of town, with its red doors open wide. The worship space is expansive with room for hundreds but set with chairs in a circle so that the small congregation feels just the right size. Candles, a prayer wall, and warm lighting make the space feel welcoming and comfortable. A huge painting of blue and gold angels overlooks the space. A connected building, which houses offices, meeting rooms, the parlor, and the kitchen, crowded with supplies, is cramped and set up railroad (or shotgun) style, so one must pass through each room to get to the next.

Rev. Donna started as rector just a couple years before my visit. A white, middle-aged woman with a passion for community, she balances the chaos of new ideas with the steadiness of maintenance. Called as priest, not a program director, Donna pressed the congregation to stand more clearly on the church side of the fuzzy line between church and social-service agency. For her, that means creating community with the people who need the services Trinity provides. The leaders of Trinity started their ministry by attending the Welcome Church, an outdoor church reaching homeless and at-risk adults, in order to build relationships and determine what the community of people who are food insecure wanted.

Donna's leadership is essential to getting the work done to make the meal. Chat and Chew has something of an "I'll do what I like" agreement for the work—each woman who comes decides what she will do to help produce dinner. Donna fills two roles that are often divided at other ministries: She builds relationships and manages the details. Donna handles the overarching challenges of enforcing the rules and managing the meal preparation, along with the minutia of whether the potatoes should be peeled or just washed, while also listening to the women's stories, connecting the women to one another, and creating space for storytelling. Donna handles it all with grace.

People in the surrounding neighborhood raised money for Trinity Memorial after a lightning strike caused a fire that destroyed the sanctuary. Following reconstruction, the congregation used the funds that remained to create four affiliated nonprofits, separate from the church, to support the needs of the community in different ways. A ministry of the church, Chat and Chew grew out of the connection to the Welcome Church; they met a group of women who were cooking together and needed a location. Chat and Chew offers an environment that allows the women to be in community with one another.

The women at Chat and Chew have many choices when it comes to food availability: They can eat at the shelter where they live, and Philadelphia has many meals programs. The meal is not what makes Chat and Chew distinctive. The way that making, sharing, and breaking bread together builds community is the point. This meal serves as a way to glimpse the kingdom of God. The earliest form of Christian gathering is re-created once a month at Trinity Memorial Church. Selena told me during dinner that the meal is "restorative." She continued, "It assists God in restoring my soul. This restores you; it makes you feel human." Chat and Chew is church.

CREATING CHURCH

Working together produces a liturgy of gathering food, breaking it apart, and sharing it, repeated ritualistically over time. At church-based food ministries, it only takes adding a blessing for our meals to recreate Jesus' parallel eucharistic actions with bread: take, bless, break, and share. We are familiar with these four actions in our Communion celebrations, but Jesus engaged in those actions each time he took bread—including the story recounted in all four Gospels of the feeding the multitudes with a few loaves and fish. Whenever we engage in those four acts, we create worship, and the community gathered for that worship is church.

Worcester Fellowship started making space for people who were food insecure because of a question that was asked at a conference I attended: "How does your church serve the community?" I had already defined our outdoor gathering for worship and a meal as church but discovered that I was not letting my church members be engaged in our mission. Looking back, I realize that my mistake was larger than that. I was identifying worship as church and the meal we ate together as a mission of the church. Without saying so, I was imagining worship and lunch as two separate activities. I probably thought the Bible study afterward was church again and then the leadership meeting after that was, well, something else. In retrospect, it's interesting to think of how easily we obtained secular grants for leadership meetings and leadership retreats but not for Sunday worship or the meal. Somehow our society has gotten to the place where it has a narrow view of Sunday liturgy as only the actions one does to be church. That is not right.

To be sure, no one reading this book thinks that worship is the only thing a church does. We all grapple with creating food ministries because we believe that the church should serve people. But if we ask ourselves *What is the difference between church and a social-service organization*, the difference we point to is worship. In today's world, worship defines church. We've limited our view until we assume that worship is the only place where God enters our community. Once a week, almost always on Sunday, we honor God in a gathering called worship, and that is what makes us church. Worship looked completely different for first-century followers of Jesus. Worship in the first century was not a gathering of people to practice a liturgy, and church was not worship. In the first century, church looked like shared ministry: People gathered to eat together, everyone serving, everyone eating.

The New Testament word translated from the Greek as *worship*—often *proskynesis*—does not mean "liturgy" or even "a gathering of the community" but rather "laying prostrate," an individual or communal act of reverence or service.[1] In the early church, worship was a way of life; people gathered not to worship but to encourage one another.[2] Living a life of worship was difficult, and so the gathering offered support for that life. Hebrews 10:24-25 reminds the early church "to provoke one another to love and good deeds, not neglecting to meet together, as is the habit of some, but encouraging one another." Scholars today describe the early church community as one that gathered for daily shared meals, prayers, and teaching.[3]

In the first century, instead of gathering for worship, the church gathered to eat. Eating together was a celebration of the nearness of the kingdom of God. In *Church in the Round: Feminist Interpretation of the Church*, Letty M. Russell suggests that for a gathering to be church it must include people at the margins of society.[4] This matches what we explored earlier; Matthew 25 shows us that to be close to Jesus we must be serving people who need food, drink, and clothing, people who are strangers, in prison, and in need of healing. While it was important to worship—honor, respect, revere—God, the focus of church in the first century was on caring for and encouraging one another. The members were interdependent—each depended on the others to get by, each trusted the others to provide what they could and to take what they needed.

In direct-service food ministries, food is given and received but not shared. In traditional church, a worship service is the central event. In contrast, shared food ministry gathers people together to work and eat and, in doing so, creates church. The church it creates is not a congregation of insiders because it reaches beyond its borders. Shared food ministry invites people in—people of all faiths, abilities, classes, and races—and includes them in the work. Together we take, bless, break, and eat the bread of life as church.

DEPENDENCE AND INTERDEPENDENCE

We often hear that food ministries create "dependence." That is, people with enough resources are concerned that easily accessible food reduces a poor person's ability or willingness to be independent and self-sufficient. Some even suggest the risk of food ministries creating dependence is so high it would be better to end the programs.[5] The evidence used for these arguments is the reality that most people who eat at meals or pick up groceries do this repeatedly; they do not come once or twice and then return to self-sufficiency.

There are several problems with this fear of creating dependence. First, the people making this argument only seem to be concerned with dependency among people who are poor. Thus, there is concern that people depend upon food pantries or meal programs and that providing food will discourage individuals from looking for work. But there is not a similar concern that tax breaks for homeowners will make people dependent on government handouts or that academic scholarships will make students unaware of the cost for college. For some reason it does not feel like businesses that provide meals, gyms, or childcare to their employees are making them more dependent. There is concern that people who are not working and who are poor will become lazy or unmotivated. There is little concern that people who are not working and are not poor, such as those who are retired or living off their investments or have chosen to be stay-at-home parents, will have the same psychological damage. Our societal concern that sharing resources leads to negative consequences somehow is only a risk for those who are poor.

For Christians, the second problem with the concern for dependence is that it is not biblical. Nothing in the Bible suggests that there are any tests that our neighbors need to pass in order for us to provide them with what they need. In the story of the sheep and the goats and in the feeding of the multitudes, there is no means testing—not faith testing or dependence testing. The stories simply teach us to feed others. Acts 6 suggests we share the duty of serving the food as well.

The third issue is more complex. It is a lack of resources—not the providing of resources—that creates dependence. The people concerned with dependence insist on the importance of independence and self-sufficiency as the alternative to dependence. We need to remember independence is an American value, not a Christian value. Our church-based ministries should be focused on interdependence—the ways that we as God's people are dependent on one another and on God.

POVERTY CAUSES DEPENDENCE

The standard story people tell about dependence goes something like this: A person who is food secure—we'll call her Beth—meets a person who is food insecure, Annette, at a meal program. They have kids about the same age, and Beth goes to her church and convinces the congregation to raise money to send Annette's kids to summer camp. Then Beth helps Annette fill out the paperwork to get Supplemental Nutrition Assistance Program (SNAP) benefits. When Beth is at Annette's apartment working on the SNAP application, she is surprised to discover

Annette has a live-in boyfriend who is not working, and they pick up food every week from a different food pantry.

If Beth's primary concern is dependence, what she may see is that Annette and her boyfriend have become dependent on nice church volunteers who do the work necessary to get them help. Why isn't the boyfriend working? Why couldn't they fill out their own application? Why don't they spend their time looking for work instead of visiting the different food ministries in the area? Beth may feel this couple is depending on her instead of finding work. Maybe by providing a "handout" of food and raising money for summer camp, Beth enabled Annette and her boyfriend and removed their need to be motivated to work.

But is it really the charity that caused Annette to be dependent on food programs and Beth's fundraising? If we remove the fear that charity causes dependence, we will have different questions. How much income is needed to cover housing, an apartment, and childcare? Are there jobs in the area providing enough income for those costs? What are the barriers to getting those jobs? What skills has Annette used previously to meet the needs of her family? Has anyone gotten to know Annette well enough to help her develop those skills?

Annette is dependent on Beth and on programs providing food because she is poor. One of the skills necessary to navigate poverty is the ability to get help where one can. Thus, people who are poor learn where and when church meals occur and which pantries allow them to get a bag of food, along with the limits and restrictions of both the meal and pantry programs. People learn that telling a good, sympathetic story will increase their chances of getting help. Two people sharing an apartment reduces the cost for each person. I know a woman who fought to get the man who beat her out of jail because when he was in jail she didn't have access to his disability benefits, and she couldn't pay the rent on their apartment.

Beth need not worry about whether she is creating dependence by helping Annette. Dependence is a problem, but it is caused by poverty, by systems preventing people from getting work, by rules that don't allow people on disability to work, and by the lack of affordable childcare and inexpensive housing. The system that allows Beth (and me) to find well-paid employment and thus have resources to share is the same system that creates low-paying jobs, part-time work, and jobs with minimal benefits.[6] Beth and I avoid being accused of dependence because of our privilege—that is, attending better schools and having strong social supports, including a parent with a college degree, which gave us the choice of going to college, which in turn gave us connections for first-time jobs, which contributed to our social capital, all of which developed into economic well-being. We can't presume that giving economic support on an ad hoc basis will overcome all the systemic challenges faced by people who are poor.

Annette's problems with accessing the food she needs is caused by the social contract developed by US culture. Why do we expect mothers to be separated from their children for paid work? Why do we lack social support systems to care for children? What systems created by this country make finding work, childcare, and affordable housing so difficult? And why is Beth, who wants to help, encouraged to critique Annette when she does not make the same choices Beth herself would make?

Liberation from dependence happens when structural barriers to necessary resources, such as housing, food, and health care, are removed. Some churches are engaged in helping their communities remove barriers to finding work, improving wages, and providing access to childcare. When I worked directly with people who did not have homes, it was important to me to be on my denomination's committee that addresses systemic poverty. The work to address systemic problems further emphasizes that our goal is creating interdependence, not independence. While we work on systemic change, we can also provide direct service, knowing that it is poverty that creates dependence, not support systems for people who are poor.

SHARING POWER AND BECOMING INTERDEPENDENT

The transactional relationship we often see in direct-service charities, where one side always the gives and the other always receives, reinforces the power of systemic oppression. The persons with excess to give becomes an authority simply because they have access to material resources. Transactional ministries automatically provide the giver with power over the receiver because the giver sets the terms that the receiver must meet. *Power-over* is the standard way that we think about power. Power-over sees relationships as unbalanced: One person has the power, and the other must do what that person says. Power-over comes with authority, with physical size, with particular roles. We recognize it by seeing that one person can correct or redirect another person. Power-over need not be intentional— if we stand behind the table portioning food for people who are waiting to be served, we have power over the portion size, whether we asked for that power or not. The alternative is not giving up power; someone will fill that role if we step away from it. The alternative is *power-with*.

Power-with happens when we work intentionally to create systems where many people have the authority to make decisions. When decisions are collaborative—and, thus, relational— the power of enforcement is distributed widely. Community norms can be challenged, and the result will be a discussion more than a reprimand. One way for portion size to be power-with is for everyone to take a turn serving. Another is to allow people to serve themselves. Power-with encourages community members to make decisions together, which is dependent on getting to know one another. Power-with says that people with material resources and people without can work together for resolution.

It is logical for those who need the material goods to respond to the power-over authority by pulling away from the oppressive force, which leads to individualism and isolation. Another response is becoming resigned to dependence. Interdependence is a better choice. Shared authority and power-with allows for us to develop shared giving and receiving. These relationships involve interdependence: connecting us to one another, to God, and to the world. Using power-with to create relational leadership is not simple, and it can result in confusion and chaos and disagreement, as we have seen in the stories from the food ministries I visited. But it is Christian. Authority by power-with is messy and incomplete. It also may feel like there are too many cooks in the kitchen—both literally and figuratively. But when authority is shared, we can create a community where the members are interdependent. Interdependence creates a church where everyone is invited to belong.

If we stick to power-over, claiming all the authority for ourselves, we will miss recognizing the chronic nature of oppression in the United States. To think we can stop providing direct-service charity in order to encourage individuals to change their behavior is to miss the ongoing nature of systemic oppression. Church can be a place that ends power-over by creating ministries based on power-with. This is not community organizing or community development but rather church-making. The definition of church changes to *being community* rather than *doing mission for* the community. Everyone who takes part is one of us, and everyone is invited to take part.

CREATING INTERDEPENDENCE

Chat and Chew provides one example of how eating and working together results in people being interconnected. Trinity Memorial Church worked with the outdoor Welcome Church in order to meet women who were food insecure or homeless. Members of Trinity Memorial hand out individual invitations to the meal just a few days in advance, usually when they see people at the Welcome Church's weekday Bible study or other similar gatherings. They are selective—only asking women to attend and trying to find a group of women who will work well together. They ask for a commitment to attend in order to get a rough number of attendees and to make space to invite new women when regulars cannot make it. Though sometimes Chat and Chew has more attendees than the members had planned for, the planning team makes it work.

Small gatherings make it easier to build connections. Over a year of monthly meals, a person could spend one meal getting to know one other person. Not everyone who comes to the meal will share deeply, but all who attend will learn more about one another over time.

Interdependence requires getting to know one another well enough to trust the people to do the work. In the first few years at Worcester Fellowship, I didn't know if volunteers would step forward to do the tasks to make lunch happen. I spent a lot of time figuring out how I could transfer the five-gallon container of hot chocolate by myself. When I admitted I needed help, people came forward to unload my car. They became trustworthy when I allowed myself to let them be in charge of making the ministry happen. I had to let go of my fear and make it clear that I was not independent of them and the help they provided. For me to trust them, I had to trust that God was leading our ministry.

Church is a place where we hope to depend upon others and for them to depend upon us. Our ministries become more like church when we build that interdependence into them. This requires that we give up independence, stop worrying about dependence, and work to make two-way relationships. Some people depend upon our ministry to get food they need, and we depend upon those same people to set up, cook, and clean up after our meals. Because we have built relationships with one another, we also depend upon one another to check in about our lives. Building community is building interdependence.

DISCUSSION QUESTIONS

1. What do you define *church*? What activities help you feel connected to others in your church?

2. What is the connection between being church and having worship? What is the connection between being church and providing food? How can you make your meal or pantry more worshipful?

3. How are people in your church interdependent with one another and with God? How can you build that interdependence in your food ministry?

ELEVEN

CREATING NETWORKS

S pilled noodles go in the compost," Stephen Yorba Patten says to the teenager holding a tray of noodles, grass, and some pebbles. The church members providing supper at Urban-Mission's Open Table in Pomona, California, arrived an hour late, and then a volunteer spilled a large tray of noodles in the courtyard on the way from her car to the kitchen. "Do you have enough remaining for dinner?" Stephen asks. The volunteer sadly shakes her head, but Stephen is unfazed. "Let's go look in the pantry for more noodles."

Her arms loaded with boxes of noodles, the embarrassed volunteer returns to the kitchen. As the volunteer boils another batch of rigatoni and elbow macaroni, Stephen introduces me to the older couple who run the food pantry. They are showing two volunteers from the church how to help shoppers select what they need. The pantry is open during Sunday dinner and on Thursdays.

Stephen takes me outside to UrbanMission's winter garden and shows volunteers from the visiting church and from the neighborhood how to cut and wash salad greens on tables next to the garden. They deliver those greens to the kitchen. At one point, a member of the kitchen crew asks, "Have you seen any of the Damien volunteers?"

"They called and said they'd be late too," Stephen replies. Damien is the local Catholic high school for boys, and they provide student volunteers every week for the meal. Stephen steps into the courtyard and recruits a few people who are waiting for the meal to set up the buffet. Two long rows of tables and folding chairs are set across the sanctuary and covered with plastic tablecloths. Someone sets up a dessert station, and another carries in a coffeepot.

At 4:50 p.m., the weekly dinner is ready. One of the volunteers makes the announcement, and people move toward the line in no particular hurry. A few finish up their food pantry shopping and drop their food in their cars before coming over to dinner. The meal is scheduled at 5:00 p.m., and the early start seems to contribute to the relaxed attitude. The high school volunteers arrive after everyone is eating and are invited to sit, but they start cleaning the kitchen instead. The church that brought dinner sits to eat, intermingling with the neighborhood eaters, leaving just one person to provide seconds on request.

Dinner is over quickly, and the many children of both the eaters and the cooks step out into the courtyard for another round of tag, while the Damien volunteers fold and stack chairs and put tables away. Another Sunday evening meal is finished.

MAKING CONNECTIONS

Stephen Yorba Patten is the Community Wellness Minister at UrbanMission. An ordained, unpaid volunteer, he oversees the food and the health ministries. He is white and bivocational, a high school teacher, with a quick smile and direct manner. Stephen grew up in the area, the son of a blue-collar carpenter. He saw the construction boom that fueled this Hispanic Pomona, California, neighborhood and the quick decline when the building stopped.

"This neighborhood gets overlooked. It has struggled, but UrbanMission is not looking for what is wrong here." Stephen points out run-down houses where people have their own gardens and where neighbors participate in the church. "We look for signs of vibrancy. We look to see what God has been doing here," Stephen explains. "You hear so much of churches dying. We are scrapping the old model, overturning it. Instead, we set out a table and have dinner. We find a way to stay relevant to the people who live here." What Stephen was working on was what Al Lopez was looking for.

Al Lopez is founding pastor of UrbanMission. He is the only paid staff of this United Church of Christ and Disciples of Christ congregation, although they are working to change that. Al was looking to create ministry that grows out of what people long for rather than implementing a top-down strategy for church planting. He was beginning this work when he got a call from a friend at Disciples Seminary Foundation.

"Do you know Stephen Yorba Patten?" the friend asked. "He's passionate about food justice and lives in Pomona. You need to get together with him."

So Stephen and Al connected, an older white man from working-class Pomona and a young Hispanic man with two toddlers. Al was impressed by Stephen's desire to live out the ministry, which matched Al's experience growing up in an immigrant congregation. They discovered they have similar charismatic backgrounds and similar present-day theologies.

Stephen feels like meeting Al was something divine. When he saw the UrbanMission campus, he said, "I think we can feed people here." The space was a deserted church with three buildings and a wall forming an inner courtyard. It had a chain-link fence around the lot parking and a garden in the lot next door. Driving by on the main road, the worn-out stucco and brick, the broken tile roof, and the gate communicate closure. From the back and from the view of the neighborhood of tiny houses, the connections between the space and the community can be seen. The gate is open, and there is a walkway into the courtyard.

Stephen has connections—connections to organizations that worked with food and connections to several high schools and the local colleges. He tells everyone he meets he is looking for partners. "I put together partners who can host dinners, dinner Sunday nights in the middle of the sanctuary." First, UrbanMission offered a Thanksgiving dinner, then an Easter dinner, and then a meal every Sunday evening. "Once we opened the doors, we couldn't close them," he said. "Every Sunday at the same time. Consistency. Bigger celebrations and parties at the holidays."

Stephen invited everyone he met to come and cook. The first meals at UrbanMission served ten to fifteen people, but now they serve fifty to seventy-five. High school students and parents volunteer together, and local college students come regularly for one term. Other organizations support the people who eat at UrbanMission in other ways. Some of the volunteers, like the nursing students who come to cook once a month, were moved by what they saw, which led to initiating the Community Wellness Center. The old parsonage was converted into a center with graduate nurses from Western University Health Sciences and women from Pomona's Health Promoters providing medical advice and health education to local families.

NETWORKING

Stephen started Open Table at UrbanMission by asking an Episcopal youth director to gather a group to cook. They offered the meal to the community and then sat down together to eat. At Worcester Fellowship, our partnerships started one Saturday night when I realized I didn't want to make any more sandwiches. I needed help. Like Stephen, I called a friend and asked if she could put together a group to provide lunch.

When we invite others into our programs, we need to teach the new volunteers that this is not a "cooks cook and eaters eat" program. It can be difficult to ease the partnering organizations into sitting and eating and inviting the eaters to join in the serving. Stephen says that the people bringing dinner often feel like outsiders. They want to be part of the community but don't know how to join. The community's job is to bring them in and figure out what they are passionate about. This circles back to the idea that we have to get to know our volunteers' needs, strengths, skills, and desires. This is true whether the volunteers are food secure or food insecure.

"One of the initial steps is soil testing. To grow an abundant crop, you have to test the soil and know what you are working with," Stephen remarks. At first, I think he is telling me about the UrbanMission garden, but he's actually talking about creating networks of people to help with ministry. "You have to ask people about their connection to the community. You have to pay attention to what resources they need and what they have to offer."

Stephen describes what he is doing as an extension of what he has always done—connecting people to one another. "Everybody in my neighborhood is in my congregation whether they know it or not, and it doesn't require that they come Sunday morning." His is an expansive view of church. Notice he does not say, "Please come help us." Networking says, "Let's work together." It means that the partners have a say in how things are done.

Stephen started with people he knew—people from the school where he works and from organizations he is part of— and those people referred him to others to create an ever-widening circle. At Worcester Fellowship, we started every new program by telling everyone we met what was needed. We told people who were food secure or insecure, funders, and mission teams; we mentioned our needs in sermons and lectures. When someone replied, "That sounds interesting to me," we began looking for ways that person could volunteer. Some said, "I can offer this specific expertise"; others asked, "What can I do to help?" Networking is the process for getting interested people connected to each other.

THREE WAYS TO NETWORK

All of the shared-ministry sites I visited are networked with other organizations and therefore multiply their impact on the community. For some, their primary networking was providing space in their building for other services and programs reaching a similar group of people. Others partner with local churches and ask its members to bring a meal or serve as volunteers. Several also work with secular organizations in a variety of ways.

OFFERING OUR SPACE TO OTHERS

The food pantry at UrbanMission is a great example of opening a space to another program. Inland Valley Hope Partners was already providing food to people in Pomona. As UrbanMission worked to get its building space usable, it welcomed the food pantry's request to set up a site on its campus. Inland Valley Hope Partners has a different set of rules than UrbanMission—most pantries have more qualifying guidelines than meals do—but they still manage to work together. St. James Church also invites many organizations to use its building, and each organization reaches different populations—youth who are homeless, people with addictions, immigrants. St. James's main hall can be adapted easily for different uses. Its couches can slide into a living room setup for discussion or can be moved into a side room when the space is full of tables.

WORKING WITH OTHER CHURCHES

The most common working partner for any church-based food ministry is other churches. Individual members volunteer at neighboring churches, and youth groups, mission teams, and other groups come from one church to do mission at another. At Worcester Fellowship, two different churches send their choirs to sing for our worship once or twice year. Georgeanne, Mary, and I would preach at morning worship in suburban churches, asking those churches for their prayers, for volunteers, and for financial support. We developed a schedule where five churches partner with us once a month (or once a quarter) to provide lunch and join us for worship. In return, we offer preaching and youth group programs. Additionally, some of our church members will visit other congregations. As the program has grown, we've added a second lunch provider each Sunday; thirty additional churches bring lunch once or twice year.

At Brighton Allston Congregational in Massachusetts and Hope Lutheran in Reading, Pennsylvania, the pastors use denominational newsletters, clergy gatherings, and judicatory meetings to find volunteers. Often a volunteer or two from one church encourages others from their congregation to come along next time. Hope asks suburban parishes to cook dinner occasionally. Youth groups and outreach committees help serve at Brighton Allston Congregational. St. James developed a weekly newsletter that is distributed to donors, volunteers, and other local churches. Worcester Fellowship, Brighton Allston, and Hope all employ a dedicated administrator who keeps the schedule, requests churches to fill open slots for cooking or volunteering, and sends out reminders.

When MANNA began in Boston, The Cathedral of St. Paul's Monday Lunch already had five churches in the rotation to cook. MANNA worked to involve the cooks in a new way of ministry. They took advantage of their location at the cathedral to draw in priests and active laypeople who were involved in diocesan

149

events. Several priests from suburban churches "stop in" regularly to visit and provide pastoral care.

Emily, the Downtown Welcome Table companion coordinator in Asheville, North Carolina, brings in most of her many individual volunteers by visiting churches and networking with local organizations. Youth groups also send volunteers to Welcome Table. A few groups come regularly and have become an integral part of the community.

CONNECTING TO SECULAR ORGANIZATIONS

Many programs also turn to secular organizations and people not connected to churches to partner with their ministries. At UrbanMission, Stephen worked with students in a graduate nursing program to create the church's health and wellness outreach program. He also found teen volunteers through their membership to social justice clubs. Haywood Street Congregation networks with local restaurants to get training in skills like bread baking or to learn a new recipe. Another meal program in town distributes leftovers from those restaurants.

Members of St. James Church heard from participants about the high rates of diabetes in their community, so their pantry emphasizes the importance of the fresh fruits, vegetables, yogurt, and milk that they provide. Staff from the food bank come to the pantry and offer nutrition advice centered around the food they are offering that day, often cooking up samples and serving them to the people waiting their turn to shop.

Brighton Allston Congregational has developed connections to the justice system; their meal and food pantries provide a place that individuals can do court-mandated volunteer service or meet parole obligations. Volunteers also come from a center for people with disabilities, from local colleges, and from neighborhood businesses. Worcester Fellowship got a grant from the Worcester Foundation—a nonprofit support organization—to create leadership training events for volunteers who don't have homes or are food insecure. Many cities have a foundation whose aim is to support local nonprofits with training and funding.

CHALLENGES IN CREATING NETWORKS

There are challenges to creating networks. A meal program must be clear on its mission and know why it wants to develop partnerships with other organizations. Not all churches will be aligned with that mission. Some secular organizations may balk at the faith-based approach, but we shouldn't invite programs into our buildings that will promote ideas that work against our values.

At Worcester Fellowship, we unknowingly scheduled two churches from the same town on the same date, which normally wouldn't have been an issue except many disgruntled parishioners had left one of the churches to attend the other. They were surprised to find themselves serving lunch together. Luckily, over the following months it turned into a moment of healing rather than more fighting, but the pastors would have appreciated a warning ahead of time. I always worried whether some of the churches that came would be distressed by the plastic bowl of condoms on the altar/table; we were sometimes asked why it was there, but no one ever followed up with a complaint. Mostly, I want all the churches connected to Worcester Fellowship to be able to work together despite potential differences in theology and politics.

Worcester Fellowship created an art program at a peer recovery center, and we hoped it would be a great collaboration. However, the peer recovery center had a rule that only sober and clean parishioners could attend. Though we understand that some ministries and outreach programs rules require sobriety, this is not the type of ministry that Worcester Fellowship provides. Eventually, we decided that we would only meet in spaces where everyone is welcome. We still refer people to the peer recovery program, but we do not host any of our events there.

MINISTRY TO PEOPLE WHO ARE FOOD SECURE

People want to care for their neighbors. By networking with other churches and with secular organizations, we provide them that opportunity. By practicing shared ministry, we hope to teach people how to be in community, to help them live into their call, and to guide them to get to know the people they want to serve. At UrbanMission, student volunteers who attend as part of a class will often return to be part of the community after the class is over. Partnerships help to expand the definition community, both for those who come to volunteer and for us. Networking brings resources together for the common good, and we are all fed by that experience.

At Worcester Fellowship, we eventually decided that one of our ministries was teaching people who have homes how to interact and build relationships with people who do not have homes. When confirmation classes came to bring lunch, we met with them in advance to describe our worship and lunch and to give advice for what they could do to start conversations. Simple discussions, such as asking people about where they live or where they grew up or what they do for fun, helped the youth recognize that they could ask the same questions of our Worcester Fellowship members as they did anyone. We also suggested that the students set a goal of learning the name of at least three people during an afternoon. We gave advice on how to engage in conversation while in line, how to start a conversation, and what to do if people want to talk to them during worship. (Ask them to step just outside the worship circle and have the conversation—but don't leave the park!)

Teens aren't the only ones who need help engaging; adults need guidance too. Many come to our meal assuming their role is to stand behind a table. But Worcester Fellowship created other roles: roving listeners, pastoral caregivers, prayer collectors. I visited a church meal where one person at each table has the role of keeping everyone included in the conversation.

Volunteers need encouragement to push beyond their comfort zone and to look for interactions they weren't expecting.

At Worcester Fellowship, we began bringing outdoor church members to Bible studies and worship at indoor churches that regularly sent volunteers. Our outdoor church members began to feel responsible for making the indoor church members feel welcome, and this made the interactions and relationship-building two-sided. Everyone felt the responsibility to make connections with people they didn't know, and this helped Worcester Fellowship become a network of connected churches instead of a ministry of one church to another.

Creating networks is part of recognizing that we are not in this ministry alone. Other organizations and other people are available to help. We do not need to be silos, each holding our work privately. We can build interdependence in our organizations. The ministry at UrbanMission is much larger than its paid staff or new church status would predict because it connects with existing community organizations. Making space for networking with our neighborhoods will grow our ministries in new and creative ways.

DISCUSSION QUESTIONS

1. How can you create networks in your community among meal programs, churches, and secular organizations? How do you see God working in your connection to other organizations?

2. How will you balance making connections to other organizations with maintaining the identity of your ministry?

3. What values of your ministry are you unwilling to change to suit another organization's rules? How will you communicate those values?

TWELVE

EATING TOGETHER
IS CHURCH

While working on my doctoral project, I call a pastor whose church offers lunch after worship to ask if I can visit. "I heard you have a lunch after church," I tell her. "I would love to see it as research for my doctoral project."

"Lunch after church?" the pastor replies. "No, we don't have lunch after church."

"Oh, sorry," I respond, embarrassed. "I must have gotten the wrong information."

Two years later, I visit that same pastor—Karen Fritz—at her church, Brighton Allston Congregational, on a Sunday morning for Bible study, worship, and social time afterward. In place of coffee and pastries, Brighton Allston offers a choice of two soups, a crusty baguette, and a slice of cake. I visit with church members, eat lunch, and then pull Karen aside. "I thought you said you didn't have a meal after church."

"We don't."

"Karen, I just ate a bowl of soup and a piece of bread. With cake. I just had lunch"

"Oh, that was just food from the pantry. Laura put it together to make a soup."

"Does Laura do that every week?"

"No, sometimes we just have sandwiches."

"So there is lunch every week after church?"

"Well, I don't really think of it as lunch. It's coffee hour for people who don't have access to enough food. But it's not a meal, you know. It's just something to eat after church."

TUESDAY AT HOPE'S TABLE

Hope Lutheran Church has upstairs church on Sunday and downstairs church on Tuesday. I visit on a Tuesday during Lent. In a well-lit basement room, about fifty people gather for Hope's Table. The group is racially diverse, and I have seen about half of the members at upstairs church the previous Sunday. Dinner opens with a prayer and an invitation to join the buffet line. Several people arrive while we are eating, and half an hour later, Mary, the priest, announces that worship will begin. A few people leave, and a few more arrive just in time for worship. Mary takes prayer requests before the service starts, writing them down and interacting with folks to get the details of their story. She had done the same on Sunday. Then the service starts. We have bulletins at our seats next to our dirty plates, but most people know the responses without looking. A group of teens lead the first song, and Mary's sermon is a dialogue in which she asks the eaters to respond to questions and share their experiences.

Two women off to the side continue their dinner conversation, occasionally laughing wildly, seemingly oblivious to the worship service, although their three children pay rapt attention to Mary. A man at the table behind me, maybe thirty years old, gets out of his seat and slowly walks toward the door. Mary has to step out of his way so he can get by, but he does not interrupt her dialogue with the congregation. At the door, the man drops a crumpled napkin into the trash and turns to walk slowly back. Mary steps aside again so he can pass without stopping her sermon, and he sits down again. After Mary offers a prayer that includes all the prayer requests from earlier, we share Communion, each person coming forward for a small piece of bread dipped in grape juice. A man arrives just as the line starts for Communion, and Mary asks if he's had dinner. He replies that he only came for church. About two-thirds of the people present come up to be served, including all the children.

Worship is followed by meal cleanup. Everyone takes their own mess to a rolling cart with bins for plates, flatware, and cups, and a volunteer takes the first batch to the kitchen to start washing. A few people organize wiping down the tables and chairs, folding them, and putting them away. Several people meet with Mary to share a story, and others leave until next time.

BIBLE STUDY

Bible study at Brighton Allston Congregational Church is on Sunday at 9:30 a.m. The disheveled meeting space is off the main social hall and contains two tired couches making an L-shape across from a few comfortable chairs. Folding chairs in the spaces between make a half circle. The coffee is off to the right on a small table; a large dining table bumps up to the circle of chairs. A mini-kitchen just off this room holds a sink, a mini-fridge, an electric kettle, and a microwave. Folks trickle into the space and are each welcomed warmly by Karen and by others in the group. On the day I visit, twelve people—men and women, white, Hispanic, and Asian—are in attendance.

The study begins with a volunteer reading aloud the story of Noah and another a passage from Mark. Karen opens with the question, "What do you think about covenant?" and three people dive into the discussion.

One man arrives late, and he takes his time getting settled. He takes off his coat, sits down, adjusts his folding chair, gets up for coffee, sits down, puts his coat back on, changes to another seat, asks if there will be cake, folds the handout and puts it in his pocket, then takes it back out. All the while keeping up with the conversation, he adds, "I can really connect to the Spirit sending Jesus into the wilderness. I guess covenant means God will take care of him."

"Do you feel like God takes care of you?" asks one of the other women.

The man puts the handout back in his pocket and pulls out tobacco to roll a cigarette. "Yeah, God is taking care of me. But it's bad now. Really bad." He puts the supplies back in his pocket. "I gotta go."

"I'm glad you could come, Jacob." Karen calls to him as he leaves. She turns back to the group. "Any other ideas for covenant?"

MEAL OR CHURCH? YES.

At both Brighton Allston Congregational Church and Hope Lutheran Church, the line between what is meal and what is worship is unclear. The line between who is a member and who is seeking ministry from the church is unclear. Both churches are deeply rooted in the people in their local communities, many who are food insecure. The food is not the most important part of what the churches offer; thus, coffee hour is not lunch—even when it includes all the food for lunch.

Brighton Allston Congregational offers Bible study, worship, and a not-meal on Sunday; dinner and Bible study on Wednesday; food pantry on Saturday; plus a thrift shop open Wednesday at lunch and Saturday mornings. The building is open on the coldest nights for emergency housing. Hope Lutheran offers Sunday worship, Tuesday dinner and worship, a Tuesday food pantry, plus programming for local youth. Both Brighton Allston and Hope Lutheran run on shoestring budgets with a full-time pastor, a part-time administrator, a part-time sexton, and a musician. Much of the pastors' work is fundraising, grant writing, and pastoral care. Volunteers, food secure and food insecure, their own church members, neighbors, and people from the suburbs run the food ministries. They are a light in neighborhoods that need signs of hope.

EATING TOGETHER AND THE EARLY CHURCH[1]

In the first few centuries of Christianity, followers of Jesus gathered to eat together. Because they shared all their resources in common, a common meal was prepared. The meal was followed by a symposium—listening and discussing scripture and other texts. The meal and discussion were a time of thanks or, in Greek, *eucharist*. For those followers who were poor, they were thankful for the community and also for the access to food.

Jesus tells us that the kingdom of God has begun with his presence. Isaiah 55:1 describes the coming kingdom as a world where everyone has enough to eat: "Everyone who thirsts, come to the waters; and you that have no money, come, buy and eat! Come, buy wine and milk without money and without price." I imagine that the chance to gather together every day and to get enough to eat felt exactly like the beginning of the kingdom of God. The church's mission of welcome included offering food to everyone.

But food-insecure people are not the only ones who find God's kingdom in shared meals. Anyone who is lonely or lost finds people they can share with. And those who wish they could give of themselves find the kingdom in the opportunity to serve others. People with plenty of material resources find God's kingdom in their ability to share their resources. The modern church is most like the early church when we gather around a meal.

Brighton Allston Congregational and Hope Lutheran are like the early church in that there is no difference between gathering for a meal and gathering for worship. These churches don't "do mission projects" but rather are communities that eat together and share groceries with one another. Some people come to meals in order to socialize with other congregants; others come to receive the food resources they wouldn't otherwise have. Church members eat and serve—some are food secure; others are food insecure. Some people leave before the Bible study or worship; some skip eating and only attend the worship or study.

These churches recognize that individuals who are food insecure want food not only for their bodies but also for their souls. These churches work to lift up everyone with words of good news, with the chance to volunteer, and with nourishment. No one has the sole responsibility to be a giver, and no one must only be a receiver. The people involved are interdependent— dependent upon one another and God.

The boundaries at both churches are porous; it is not clear who is a member and who is not. Community neighbors are active in the meals, the food pantry, and in the worship and Bible studies, whether or not they have officially joined the church. Church members come to some events and not others and are sometimes volunteers and sometimes recipients. But there is always plenty to eat and plenty of community, and that's good news. These churches have succeeded in creating interdependent communities that practice evangelism—that is, they invite new people in for worship, music, and celebration. People volunteer to be refreshed and lifted up as well as to care for others.

EVANGELISM

Like mission, evangelism is not a project but rather a way of being for the church. Though Brighton Allston and Hope Lutheran do not impose lines between who is "in" and who is "out" of church, they do reach out to local neighbors, asking them to join for meals, studies, and worship. Evangelism, we must remember, is the sharing of good news. Luke 4:18-19 reminds us of Jesus' words:

> "The Spirit of the Lord is on me,
>   because he has anointed me

> to bring good news to the poor.
> He has sent me to proclaim release to the captives
> and recovery of sight to the blind,
> to let the oppressed go free,
> to proclaim the year of the Lord's favor."

Thus a church acts as the body of Christ when it publicly proclaims good news to the poor. Good news comes in the form of food, support, and a chance to create new relationships. Evangelism does not ask people to believe particular doctrines but invites them to be part of a community. Evangelism says, "You belong." In this way, church-based food ministries practice evangelism. Because of our faith in Christ, we choose to provide food for people who are food insecure. We choose to make space for people to join us in this mission, to become one of us in this community. In so doing, we practice shared ministry and provide everyone with opportunities to volunteer. When we do these things, the food program becomes church.

Some churches avoid faith language in their food ministries as a way to make clear that they do not require a specific statement of faith from people for them to be permitted to eat. The problem with this is it communicates that eaters and people who are food insecure are not welcome in the churches' faith discussions or as members of those churches. These churches fail to proclaim good news because they fail to tell their own faith story and fail to listen to the faith stories of others. On the other hand, some churches engage in food ministries as a way to convert eaters to specific faith doctrines. This practice discounts the idea that people who are food insecure are already people of deep faith. While their faith does not always end addictions, mental health challenges, or poverty, it does support them in their struggles. To not recognize their faith journeys is to fail to proclaim the good news that Jesus walks with us in our hard times.

Evangelism can—must—be done *with* others rather than *to* them. Shared ministry engages in evangelism by building long-lasting relationships, by sharing faith, and by learning from others' faith. It requires recognizing that people who seek additional resources may feel unworthy—not because they do not have gifts or do not have faith but because stereotypes have encouraged them to see systemic barriers as their own fault. Shared ministry engages in evangelism through eating together and working together so that all can recognize the strengths and skills they have been given by a gracious and loving God.

OTHER EXAMPLES OF BEING CHURCH

Many of the other church-based food ministries I visited are living out the idea that sharing food is church. St. James offers worship six days a week, and the services are scheduled to accommodate the various ministries of the church. The thrift store is a community, as is the meal and the food pantry. Each of these communities overlaps each other and overlaps with the Sunday worshiping community. As we saw earlier, MANNA became church when the leadership team decided to move worship into the same space as the meal. Haywood Street Congregation offers worship following both its Wednesday and Sunday meals.

UrbanMission and Trinity Memorial Church have Sunday worship that is not explicitly connected to their meals or food pantry. Still, their meal programs have spiritual components that make clear they are ministries of churches and not social services. While social-service ministries are about meeting people's material needs, church asks how we can find and create God's kingdom together.

GETTING STARTED

In the formula Jesus offered at meals of *taking, blessing, breaking,* and *sharing* bread, turning a meal into worship requires only adding a *blessing*. This blessing sends the message of intentionality, inviting all volunteers to think about the meal as worship. What would *bless* the way we serve, the way we chat, the way we clean up? How can we make it easier for people to see that the bread is blessed, broken, and shared? At one church I visited, the volunteers made a big deal about scooping leftovers into take-out containers and holding the hands of people who took their food with them. It felt like the end of worship, this sending of people out to eat and proclaim good news.

It is also fairly simple to add a worship or study component to any food pantry or meal program. Worship can be done ahead of the meal or following it. At Hope Lutheran, worship started after just half an hour of eating and the cleanup was left for afterward. At MANNA, worship setup was part of meal cleanup. Most churches found that they had better attendance if they schedule worship close to the start or end time of the meal or pantry. Volunteers can be included in planning the worship, and they can be given leadership roles in the service as well. For those programs with leadership teams, Bible study could be a part of team meetings or could be done before or after the meeting. At Worcester Fellowship, we encouraged people to come to Bible study by buying coffee for those who attended. While that certainly meant some people came only for the coffee, it led to a wide diversity of participants and deep conversations about faith. In a community with several meal programs that also offered Bible studies, MANNA decided to offer something slightly different. MANNA started teaching spiritual disciplines such as meditation to provide a break from the noisiness of life on the streets.

Worship services or Bible studies can be started as a trial run. Make announcements about a month in advance about when the service or study will begin. Those who seem especially interested may want to join a leadership team to help plan the gathering. After the first worship or Bible study, leave a short time for evaluation. Have a specific list of questions—was the service too long or too short? Did people know the music and take part? Was it too wordy, was the language understandable?

For a Bible study, did everyone who wanted to get to share? Take notes and gather the planning team again to discuss all these answers.

Worcester Fellowship had around six people attending worship for months after we started. We began many worship services singing, "This is the *group* that the Lord has made" instead of "This is the *day* that the Lord has made." Eventually we had twelve people for worship, but many did not show up on time. After about a year, twenty people would attend, and I remember thinking to myself, *We are finally church.*

Worcester Fellowship's Bible study had a much rockier start. We started meeting in the public library in one of its reserved rooms, but a worker asked us to leave because we were noisy. Then we moved to a coffee shop, and for a year maybe two or four people would attend—sometimes only one. I was about to quit doing it altogether when the coffee shop we met in closed for construction. But one of the regulars (meaning he came every two or three weeks) suggested we move to the local hospital atrium near the coffee shop. I reluctantly agreed to try it for another month. It was the perfect spot. Over the next year, it grew to ten and sometimes fifteen people. The second year, it grew to thirty, and we had to split into two groups. Once around ten people began coming regularly, the fights about theology started. People would declare that they knew what the texts meant and would argue with anyone who said differently. We changed the question we asked about scripture to, "What does this text tell you to do in your life?" from "What does this text mean?" We also began going around the circle, allowing each person to speak or pass. This prevented anyone from taking over the discussions.

As with any new program at church, creating something new requires finding the right time and the right space for it to be successful—and then waiting the right amount of time for it to catch on. The goal is to be a community that is connected to Jesus. When we begin to feel frustrated or start losing hope, we can remind ourselves how we are connected to Jesus and to one another. We can remember that we are the church. Trying something new is worth it if it helps us get to know what it means to follow Jesus together.

DISCUSSION QUESTIONS

1. What does being church mean to you? to your congregation? What can you add to your mission to make it more church-like?

2. How does your food ministry practice evangelism? What good news are you sharing? How do you convey the good news?

3. Which of your church's activities are most similar to the early church gatherings? In the first century, having enough food was a sign of the start of the kingdom of God. What would be a sign of the start of the kingdom of God in your community today?

GO OUT INTO THE WORLD

S hortly after Alan died, I left Worcester Fellowship. I needed time to work on my doctorate, I needed a break from the chaos, and, to be honest, I needed a break from God. What good is a God who doesn't take care of people like Alan? Would it have been that hard for God to come up with a better ending to his story?

As I visited the churches mentioned in this book, I became reenergized for ministry. I also found that pastors and volunteers everywhere spend some time angry at God. Sticking with this type of work requires self-care: taking breaks from time to time, keeping healthy boundaries, attending Al-Anon meetings, joining support groups, going on vacation. It requires talking to others who are doing this work, naming the frustrations, and letting them go. It also takes reminding ourselves why we do this work. Shared ministry's goal is not to fix people; rather, its goal is to create church with people who are different from us. Church is not where everything is perfect; it is where everything is real. It isn't a solution to homelessness or poverty or addiction or mental health challenges. Church is where all these issues are recognized as systemic problems of our society, not judgments on the people they impact. Church is where we love people for who they are. Church connects us to other people, and those connections help us find Jesus.

The church must clearly be a place where Christ is present. Our churches must be open to being transformed by the people we interact with, and we must learn to see the systems that create poverty and how we are part of those systems. Somehow, we each must learn how to be transformed by meeting people like Alan and yet not be destroyed when their lives are not suddenly improved by our presence. We will be wounded but hopefully not broken when their lives end.

Alan taught me things that, at some gut level, I already knew—things that most Christians know as well. We know that all Christians are called to be disciples, to be ministers of the church. We know that giving to others helps us feel valuable and important. We know the importance of welcoming all kinds of people into church—not just people who look like us. Yet we create ministries that forget all these things we know. We don't do this because we are unkind or unthoughtful but because we are modeling what others before us have done. But we have the power to change our ministries. We can share our ministry with our neighbors.

The ministries I visited decided to prioritize making space for the people who ate in their programs and the people who shopped for food to be volunteers. They asked for their input and valued their wisdom. They invited them in and let them lead. They recognized that Jesus is in the people our ministries serve and decided they wanted to get to know Jesus. We can do these things in our congregations as well by choosing a shared-ministry approach. Once we prioritize people over efficiency and relationships over order, we will always have more than enough volunteers.

I insisted this should be a "how-to" book. I want people to create shared ministry in their own congregations. But writing a how-to book presumes a step-by-step approach to engaging in ministry. No such approach exists. Every location, every gathering of people is unique. Our contexts will determine what we can and should do and how we proceed. But regardless of our context, we can begin by paying attention to the people and communities around us—especially to those who are food insecure.[1] Then, we can build relationships with these people, eventually asking them to lead our programs or to lead us in discerning the next steps we need to take. We can make space to bless the bread we share and space for people to bless one another. If we follow these steps, connections will inevitably form, creating church.

Stephen Yorba Patten at UrbanMission told me that he started with food because food is both a struggle for people and a necessity. "There is so much about food—the way it's grown, the symbolism, food in the gospel," Stephen explained. "There is something important that extends from the Communion table. Christians, regardless of their background, have always found a way to meet around that table. That's probably the oldest tradition we can go back to, all the way back to first-century Christianity, sitting at table and breaking bread. This sitting and breaking is the core of the gospel."

Eating together with hospitality so radical that we ask our neighbors to help us set up or clean up builds relationships. We take bread, bless it, break it, and distribute it to all who are gathered. We recognize the brokenness of our world, where we are separated from one another and from God, and, at the same time, celebrate the bounty we share together. The shared bread and shared work turn neighbors into friends. "This is not rocket science; anyone can do it. Everyone can do it. It hits at the heart of every person's experience," Stephen told me. "Don't let your church kitchen go to waste."

I learned so much from visiting shared-ministry kitchens and pantries, but what became clear was that very ordinary people created these ministries. We all have the ability to create a food program where we can work, eat, and thank God together. We can get to know people who are food insecure in our communities, find out the needs and strengths of our neighbors, and begin to feed one another. In fact, perhaps our greatest resource is someone who says, "I see a hungry crowd, and I have five loaves of bread and two fish that I am willing to share." I am confident that God will help us figure out what to do next.

DISCUSSION QUESTIONS

1. Describe any similarities between your church and the churches described in this book. Describe any differences. How do the similarities or differences affect how you will create or run a food ministry?

2. How are you caring for yourself as you engage in ministry? How can you support other volunteers in practicing self-care? What biblical images remind you to take care of yourself?

3. What is standing in the way of your congregation engaging in shared ministry? How can you help people see the benefits? What is God calling you to do next?

CHURCHES MENTIONED

A summary of the churches and people I visited and wrote about in Five Loaves, Two Fish, Twelve Volunteers.

Food for All is a ministry of St. James's Church with a meal, a food pantry, a thrift store, and several other ministries that rent their building. Pastor Paula Green is the pastor, and Andrea, who is food insecure, serves as the pantry director. Coffee Bill was a volunteer in 2016.

Open Table (Pomona, California) is a ministry of UrbanMission. UrbanMission is a new church affiliated with the United Church of Christ and Christian Church (Disciples of Christ). The Rev. Al Lopez serves as the lead pastor. The Rev. Stephen Yorba Patten serves as the community wellness minister. I visited in 2018. www.umpomona.org.

Downtown Welcome Table (Asheville, North Carolina) is a ministry of Haywood Street Congregation. It is affiliated with The United Methodist Church. The Rev. Brian Coombs is the founding pastor. Dave Holland serves as the banquet steward. Emily Bentley Pettigrew was the companion coordinator when I visited in 2018. haywoodstreet.org.

Chat and Chew (Philadelphia, Pennsylvania) is a ministry of Trinity Memorial Church, an Episcopal Congregation, and The Welcome Church, a Lutheran church that worships outside. The Rev. Donna Maree is the rector of Trinity. www.trinityphiladelphia.org. The Rev. Schaunel Steinnagel is associate pastor of The Welcome Church. Selena was part of Chat and Chew when I visited in 2016. www.thewelcomechurch.org.

Hope's Table and Hope Pantry (Reading, Pennsylvania) are ministries of Hope Lutheran Church, an ELCA Congregation. Rev. Mary Wolfe is the pastor. I visited in 2018. readinglutheranparish.org/hope-lutheran-church/.

Worcester Fellowship (Worcester, Massachusetts) is an outdoor church affiliated with the United Church of Christ and the Christian Church (Disciples of Christ). The Rev. Dr. Elizabeth Mae Magill and Mary Jane Eaton are the founding pastors. Rev. Georgeanne Bennett was the outreach minister while Alan was a volunteer. www.worcesterfellowship.org.

Brighton Allston Congregational Church (Brighton, Massachusetts) is affiliated with the United Church of Christ. They have a community supper, a food pantry, and not-lunch after church on Sundays. The Rev. Karen Fritz was the pastor when I visited in 2018. David Husselbee, Kathleen Babbin, Karen Essrow, Sister Maggie Kilduff, and Ladouceur Marie Lourdy are among the many regular volunteers at the pantry. brightonucc.org.

Many Angels Needed Now and Always (MANNA) (Boston, Massachusetts) is a ministry of The Cathedral Church of St. Paul (Episcopal). The Rev. Canon Cristina Rathbone (Tina) was the pastor and then the canon missioner of MANNA when I visited in 2016 and again in 2018. www.stpaulboston.org/.

FOR FURTHER READING

Bouman, Stephen P. *The Mission Table: Renewing Congregation and Community*. Minneapolis: Augsburg Fortress, 2013.

de la Peña, Matt. *Last Stop on Market Street*. Illustrated by Christian Robinson. New York: G. P. Putnam's Sons, 2015.

Ekblad, Bob. *Reading the Bible with the Damned*. Louisville, KY: Westminster John Knox Press, 2005.

Gutiérrez, Gustavo. *We Drink from Our Own Wells: The Spiritual Journey of a People*. 20th Anniversary edition. Translated by Matthew J. O'Connell. Maryknoll, NY: Orbis Books, 2003.

Mather, Michael. *Having Nothing, Possessing Everything: Finding Abundant Communities in Unexpected Places*. Grand Rapids, MI: Wm. B. Eerdmans Publishing, 2018.

Miles, Sara. *Jesus Freak: Feeding, Healing, Raising the Dead*. San Francisco: Jossey-Bass, 2010.

Rennebohm, Craig with David Paul. *Souls in the Hands of a Tender God: Stories of the Search for Home and Healing on the Streets*. Boston: Beacon Press, 2008.

NOTES

INTRODUCTION

1. Andrew Fisher, *Big Hunger: The Unholy Alliance between Corporate America and Anti-Hunger Groups* (Cambridge, MA: The MIT Press, 2017), 7.
2. Alisha Coleman-Jensen, Matthew P. Rabbitt, Christian A. Gregory, and Anita Singh, Household Food Security in the United States in 2017, ERR-256, U.S. Department of Agriculture, Economic Research Service, 6.
3. Fisher, *Big Hunger*, 17–18.
4. Christine Borger, Amaris Kinne, Meghan O'Leary, Sheila Zedlewski, Emily Engelhard, Jill Montaquila, Elaine Waxman, et. al, *Hunger in America 2014: Executive Summary* (Feeding America, August 2014), 3. http://www.feedingamerica.org/hunger-in-america/our-research/hunger-in-america/hia-2014-executive-summary.pdf.

CHAPTER ONE: FEEDING JESUS

1. Rudolf Brändle, "This Sweetest Passage: Matthew 25:31-46 and Assistance to the Poor in the Homilies of John Chrysostom," *Wealth and Poverty in Early Church and Society*, trans. Dan Holder, ed. Susan R. Holman (Grand Rapids, MI: Baker Academic, 2008), 133.
2. Andrew McGowan, "The Hungry Jesus," *Biblical History Daily*, Biblical Archeology Society, 03/18/2015. http://www.biblicalarchaeology.org/daily/ biblical-topics/Bible-interpretation/the-hungry-jesus/.
3. One resource for this is Bob Ekblad, *Reading the Bible with the Damned* (Louisville, KY: Westminster John Knox Press, 2005).

CHAPTER TWO: PROBLEMS WITH DIRECT-SERVICE CHARITY

1. Among the many who have explored this are Robert D. Lupton, *Toxic Charity: How Churches and Charity Hurt Those They Help (And How*

to Reverse It) (New York: HarperOne, 2011); Steve Corbett and Brian Fikkert, *When Helping Hurts: How to Alleviate Poverty without Hurting the Poor . . . and Yourself* (Chicago: Moody Publishers, 2012); Jayakumar Christian, *God of the Empty-Handed: Poverty, Power and the Kingdom of God*, rev. ed. (Victoria, Australia: Acorn Press, 2011); Kevin Blue, *Practical Justice: Living Off-Center in a Self-Centered World* (Downers Grove, IL: InterVarsity Press, 2016).

2. Borger et al., *Hunger in America*, 18.
3. Ronette Briefel, Jonathan Jacobson, Nancy Clusen, Teresa Zavitsky, Miki Satake, Brittany Dawson, and Rhoda Cohen, *The Emergency Food Assistance System—Findings from the Client Survey, Final Report*. E-FAN-03-007 by Mathematica Policy Research, Inc. for the U.S. Department of Agriculture, Economic Research Service, July 2003, 38, 87. http://www.ers.usda.gov/media/1805896/efan03007.pdf.
4. Blue, *Practical Justice*, chapters 6 and 7; Fisher, *Big Hunger*, 20.
5. Borger et al., *Hunger in America*, 8.
6. Laura Stivers, *Disrupting Homelessness: Alternative Christian Approaches* (Minneapolis, MN: Fortress Press, 2011), 58, 73, 80, 82, Kindle.
7. Stivers, *Disrupting Homelessness*, 34, 81.
8. Christian, *God of the Empty-Handed*, 2728, 2779, Kindle. Corbett and Fikkert use the idea to talk about an individual sense of superiority in *When Helping Hurts*, 61. Both note that we are not trying to be superior; we fall into this unintentionally.

CHAPTER THREE: LISTENING

1. Sara Miles, *Take This Bread: A Radical Conversion* (New York: Ballantine Books, 2007), 134–35.

CHAPTER FOUR: CULTURAL CONFLICT

1. Information on first-century worship comes from Andrew B. McGowan, *Ancient Christian Worship: Early Church Practices in Social, Historical, and Theological Perspective* (Grand Rapids, MI: Baker Academic, 2014); and from Reta Halteman Finger, *Of Widows and Meals: Communal Meals in the Book of Acts* (Grand Rapids, MI: Wm. B. Eerdmans Publishing, 2007).
2. Finger, *Of Widows and Meals*, 238–39.
3. Finger, *Of Widows and Meals*, 232.
4. Finger, *Of Widows and Meals*, 256.
5. Bruce J. Malina and John J. Pilch, *Social-Science Commentary on the Book of Acts* (Minneapolis, MN: Fortress Press, 2008), 56.

6. Find a postcolonial interpretation of this cultural conflict from Korean and Cuban perspectives in Hansung Kim, "Rereading Acts 6:1-7: Lessons for Multicultural Mission Organizations," *Evangelical Missions Quarterly* 45, no. 1 (January 2009): 56–63; and in Justo L. González, "Reading from My Bicultural Place: Acts 6:1-7," *Reading from This Place*, vol. 1, *Social Location and Biblical Interpretation in the United States*, eds. Fernando F. Segovia and Mary Ann Tolbert (Minneapolis, MN: Fortress Press, 1995).
7. McGowan, *Ancient Christian Worship*, 160, 203.
8. McGowan, *Ancient Christian Worship*, 242.
9. Robert W. Wall, "The Acts of the Apostles: Introduction, Commentary, and Reflections," in *The New Interpreter's Bible,* vol. 10, ed. Leander Keck et al. (Nashville, TN: Abingdon Press, 2002), 111.
10. Elisabeth Schüssler Fiorenza, *In Memory of Her: A Feminist Theological Reconstructions of Christian Origins*, 10th ed. (New York: Crossroad Publishing Company, 1994), 166.
11. Fiorenza, *In Memory of Her*, 165.

CHAPTER SEVEN: LET VOLUNTEERS LEAD

1. Chris Stapleton and Mike Henderson, "Broken Halos," Mercury Nashville, track one on *From a Room: Volume 1*, 2017.

CHAPTER NINE: UNEXPECTED LEARNINGS

1. Elizabeth Mae Magill, *The Theology and Practice of Sharing Ministry with Those in Need* (Fort Worth, TX: Brite Divinity School, 2017), 126.

CHAPTER TEN: INTERDEPENDENCE

1. McGowan, *Ancient Christian Worship*, 6.
2. Mike Graves, *Table Talk: Rethinking Communion and Community* (Eugene, OR: Cascade Books, 2017), 109.
3. McGowan, *Ancient Christian Worship;* Finger, *Of Widows and Meals*; and Graves, *Table Talk* makes the same point from a church development perspective.
4. Letty Russell, *Church in the Round: Feminist Interpretation of the Church,* 1st ed. (Louisville, KY: Westminster John Knox Press, 1993), 25.
5. Lupton, *Toxic Charity*, 55, and Corbett and Fikkert's *When Helping Hurts,* 102, suggest that churches stop doing direct-service charity unless the need is short-term or traumatic. Kevin Blue, *Practical Justice,* 634, Kindle, takes a more nuanced approach but also

suggests that getting resources for free can make some people not want to work.

6. Gustavo Gutiérrez, *A Theology of Liberation History, Politics, and Salvation*, 15th ed., trans. Sr. Caridad Inda and John Eagleson (Maryknoll, NY: Orbis, 1988), 52–53. Gutiérrez looks at the systems that make it so developing countries provide natural resources to first-world developers, who in turn make large profits. Fisher, *Big Hunger*, 95, shows how food businesses get tax write-offs for donating their waste to food banks while paying low salaries to workers, leaving them dependent on food pantries.

CHAPTER TWELVE: EATING TOGETHER IS CHURCH

1. This section is informed by McGowan's *Ancient Christian Worship* and Finger's *Of Widows and Meals*.

CONCLUSION: GO OUT INTO THE WORLD

1. Russell, *Church in the Round*, 32.